The
OWNER'S
MANUAL

Why, When, and How to Sell
Your Business to Private Equity

SETH DEUTSCH

Creator of the Exit Value Realization System^{TM}

The
OWNER'S
MANUAL

Why, When, and How to Sell
Your Business to Private Equity

This book is dedicated to my immediate family:
Nadia, Samson (Sammy), Delilah (DD), Blue, Daffodil, and all of the dogs
that will bless our lives. I never thought I would do this, but I relied heavily
on their strength.
This book is also dedicated to my chosen family:
Jordan, Chris, George, Peter, Tim, Bobby, and the entire clan at S&G Diner.
Thank you for your support and encouragement.
To our contributors:
Thank you for sharing your stories. It means so much to me.
And to all who read these pages: I genuinely hope this helps you. If even one
person achieves what they want through this book, then it was worth it.
P.S. SS asked that I include this poem because it's what I am doing, and I
know so many founders do the same:

The Way It Is

By William Stafford

There's a thread you follow. It goes among things that change. But it
doesn't change.

People wonder about what you are pursuing.

You have to explain about the thread.

But it is hard for others to see.

While you hold it you can't get lost.

Tragedies happen; people get hurt or die; and you suffer and get old.

Nothing you do can stop time's unfolding.

You don't ever let go of the thread.

CONTENTS

Thank You to Our Contributors

In order of appearance throughout this book:

- Adam E. Coffey, author of *The Private Equity Playbook, The Exit Strategy Playbook,* and *Empire Builder*
- Dave Rauch, Founder & CEO, ProTec Building Services
- Ryan Sprott, Co-Founder, Great Range Capital
- Christopher Geier, CEO and Managing Partner, Sikich
- Roy Bejarano, Founder and CEO, Scale Healthcare
- Lauren Von Mingee, CEO, Quintessa Marketing
- Andy Kvesic, CEO, Aprio Legal
- Brick Thompson, Co-Founder of Data & Analytics Firm, Blue Margin Inc.
- Steve Carroll, CEO & Co-founder, Kelso Industries
- Quinn Carlson, Uplift Partners
- David Harvey, Founder and CEO, Harvey and Company
- Chris Santiago, CEO, Repairs Unlimited
- Brendan Burke, Managing Director, Capstone Partners
- Steve East, Chairman, CSM Group
- Nicki Lambropoulos, CEO, Physician Directed Partners
- Gary Modrow, CFO, True Sports Group
- Gary Baughman, Partner, Samson Partners Group
- Bryan Bloom, CPA, Owner/CEO, Howard, Nunn, & Bloom
- Jordan McMillian, Partner, Samson Partners Group
- Matt Matros, Serial Entrepreneur
- Troy Kent, CEO, Kent Power
- Jim Probst, President, SBE Odyssey
- Tom Lenfestey, CEO, The Law Practice Exchange
- Ken Grider, Senior Managing Director, Raymond James
- Michael Schodrof, Vice President, Raymond James

FOREWORD

By Adam E. Coffey, author of The Private Equity Playbook, The Exit Strategy Playbook, *and* Empire Builder

In the world of business, choosing to sell your company is one of the most consequential decisions you can ever make. As someone who has lived inside private equity for decades, I know the mix of excitement, fear, pride, and uncertainty that comes with that moment. It's why I'm thrilled to introduce *The Owner's Manual: Why, When, and How to Sell Your Business to Private Equity.*

Seth and I became instant friends years ago and teammates soon after. We've advised companies together, sat on boards together, and helped founders achieve the exits they deserve. I watched him take a business from roughly $1 million of EBITDA to more than $30 million, then guide it to a blockbuster private-equity transaction. That happened in about two years. It was extraordinary work, and it wasn't a one-off. Seth has been helping CEOs and founders in public, private, and PE-backed companies do this for decades.

In recent years, he has also become one of North America's leading experts at helping law-firm founders prepare for and realize outstanding exits. As private equity fully wakes up to the opportunity in that sector, Seth and his team at Samson are positioned to help thousands of founders capture the value they've built.

Seth has helped owners realize value as a CEO, as a board member, and as a strategic advisor. At his core, though, Seth is still a coach. He takes more satisfaction from unlocking other people's potential than from anything he could do alone. Years ago, I challenged him to teach what he knows, to put his playbook in the hands of the owners who need it most. He took that challenge, built Samson, and spent two years formalizing the Exit Value Realization System (EVRS)™. Now he has translated that system into this narrative guide, turning a complex journey into simple, actionable steps any owner can follow. That's mastery.

This book is more than a guide. It's a roadmap that empowers owners to make clear, informed decisions about selling to private equity. Seth demystifies timing, preparation, deal structure, and what buyers actually value. He shows you how to see your company the way investors will see it—and how to close the gap between today's reality and tomorrow's valuation.

Inside *The Owner's Manual* you'll find practical advice, field-tested frameworks, and real-world stories. You'll learn how to assess readiness, how to build leadership and process depth that survives diligence, how to improve the quality of finance and accounting, and how to navigate the deal timeline with confidence. You'll also learn how to evaluate potential partners, not just on price, but on fit, values, and their ability to help you create the second and third bites of the apple.

What sets this book apart is its relentless focus on the owner's perspective. Selling a business is not just a financial event. It's personal. It touches your legacy, your team, and your vision for the next chapter of your life. Seth writes with empathy but stays rooted in reality. He will challenge you to look at your company through an investor's lens and then give you the tools to make it better.

Whether you plan to sell in six months or in five years, this book will meet you where you are. It distills complex concepts into clear actions and gives you a way to measure progress. Read it to get smart on what private equity is looking for. Use it to raise your multiple, improve your terms, and increase the certainty of closing the transaction. Most of all, use it to make decisions that align with your goals.

If you're an owner considering a sale, you don't need hype. You need a process, a partner, and a plan. You'll find all three here.

Here's to your success and to the opportunities that open when you take control of your exit.

VOICES FROM THE DEAL TABLE

This book features twenty-four in-depth interviews with leaders at the heart of lower-middle market private equity deals:

➡ owner-operators building companies with the objective of selling,

➡ founders and executives who have already exited,

➡ investment bankers who represent them, and

➡ private equity professionals who acquire and scale them.

Together, they show us what makes a business valuable, credible, and transactable. The conversations span industries including home services, data and analytics, manufacturing, legal, construction, route-based blue-collar services, accounting, and professional services, with perspectives from both founders preparing for exit and CEOs leading active acquisition strategies.

Drawn from real and recent experience, these interviews reflect the current landscape of private equity and bring the book's frameworks to life, painting a clear picture of what it truly takes to sell successfully to private equity today.

PROLOGUE

By Seth Deutsch, Founder of Samson Partners Group and creator of the
Exit Value Realization System (EVRS)ᵀᴹ

Like everyone, I learned about reality the hard way. As a child, I suffered severe trauma, and as a teenager, I thought basketball would be my future. I trained, sacrificed, and built my whole identity around playing in college, then professionally, then coaching. That was the plan.

While basketball gave me discipline, drive, and the dream of building something bigger than myself, it also showed me how quickly plans collide with reality. Injuries ended my college playing career before it really began, taking me from the court to the bench. At first, that shift felt like failure. What I discovered instead was one of the greatest gifts of my life: the perspective of a coach. The coach can't step on the court. A coach wins by designing the system, setting the standards, building the structure, and trusting the people to perform.

That shift—from a dream to a reality to a structure—wasn't easy, but I'm grateful for it every day. Identity is fragile; it can shatter with one bad diagnosis, one lost contract, or one broken promise. Structure endures. Structure creates results. In basketball, that means putting players in a position to succeed. In business, it means building organizations that can thrive without the founder at the center. My job, then and now, is to help people see the truth of where they are, design the right structure, and build toward the future they want.

I didn't open this prologue with a discussion of multiples or term sheets. I started with reality because selling your business is not about wishful thinking or motivational slogans. It's about seeing your company the way a buyer will. That means letting go of personal narrative, nostalgia, and self-talk. Buyers don't pay for stories; they pay for systems, numbers, people, and processes they can trust (which all, in the end, boil down to the predictability of future cash flow). When you can see your business through that lens, you not only avoid disappointment—you set yourself up to succeed.

If you're holding this book, you're likely considering selling to private equity, a strategic buyer, or another investor. Maybe you want to retire, de-risk, or scale beyond your own resources. All of those are valid goals. But no matter your reason, the outcome depends on your ability to see clearly.

My promise to you in these pages is the same promise I've always made as a coach: I won't step on the court for you, but I'll help you design the system that lets you win. And I'm grateful for the chance to walk alongside you as you take this next step.

Why This Book Exists

This book is written for small and midsized companies that don't always have access to the resources larger corporations take for granted. At Samson Partners Group, we've spent decades working with founders, owners, and private equity firms to scale and exit businesses. Almost every week, I sit across the table from founders who are about to take their business to market without being fully prepared. Sometimes they have unrealistic expectations about the price. Other times, they aren't clear on why they're selling in the first place.

When I see that, I always wish we could rewind the clock. I wish we could give that owner the tools and guidance to prepare earlier, to strengthen the business, to maximize value, and to avoid the pain of an outcome that disappoints. That wish is what drove me to create this book—and our operating system, the Exit Value Realization System (EVRS). We'll never have the chance to personally coach all the businesses that need our help. But we can provide those lessons here so you don't have to walk into a sale unprepared.

The Landscape You're Entering

To understand why preparation matters so much, it helps to zoom out. There are roughly 34 million small businesses in the U.S. Of those, only about 7% make it to $1 million in revenue. Fewer than 1% ever reach $10 million. As of late 2024, about 209,000 companies had annual sales greater than $10 million. That's a small pool compared to the total number of businesses.

And yet, those in the lower-middle market are the very companies private equity firms often pursue. In 2024 alone, private equity closed more than 8,000 acquisitions. About 74% of those deals were "add-ons"—smaller businesses folded into larger platforms. Only about 20% were "platform investments," where a company becomes the cornerstone of a roll-up strategy.

Think about the funnel this creates. To close those 8,000 deals, PE firms probably approached more than 800,000 business owners. They may have signed NDAs and done early diligence on at least 80,000. And only a fraction closed. Of the ones that did, not every owner walked away with the outcome he or she imagined at the outset. Many left money on the table, got stuck in burdensome earnouts, or saw their deal terms shift late in the process.

That's the reality of this market. The odds aren't generous, and the margin for error is small. But here's the good news: when you understand how buyers evaluate companies, when you prepare deliberately, you can shift those odds in your favor.

Operators, Not Theorists

One of the things that makes Samson different is that our team has lived in both worlds. We've been founders, executives, and operators who built and exited companies. And we've been deal partners, helping private equity firms decide which companies to buy and how to price and structure deals. We're from the arena, not the stands. We've been in your seat.

That dual perspective is powerful. On the investor side, the playbook is simple: buy the business, install structure, execute growth, exit in three to seven years with a strong return. On the founder side, the stakes feel very different: this is your life's work, your identity, your team, your family's financial future. Our job is to help you bridge those worlds—to see your business the way an investor does, and to prepare it so you can achieve the outcome you want.

The Exit Value Realization System (EVRS)™

We built Samson's EVRS™ as a practical, repeatable system for owner-led, lower middle-market companies. It asks three simple questions:

1. **Where are you now?** Baseline the business as an investor would—no spin.

2. **Where are you going?** Define the exit you want: who buys you, why, and on what terms.

3. **How do you close the gap?** Sequence and execute the initiatives that move you toward that outcome.

Simple questions. But answering them requires clarity, courage, and commitment.

In most businesses we assess, the drivers of value are easy to identify. We call them the **seven foundations of value creation**. Rarely does a company need to overhaul all seven. Usually, it's one to three areas that must improve before founders can achieve the exit they want.

The seven foundations are:

- ➡ **Vision and Strategy** – not just where you've been, but where an investor can take the business next.

- ➡ **Human Capital and Leadership** – reduce dependency on the founder, build a second line, and show the company runs without you.

- ➡ **Quality of Revenue and Growth** – diversify customers, build recurring revenue, create pricing power, and professionalize sales.

- ➡ **Quality of Operations** – document processes, measure results, expand margins, and make the machine run tighter.

- ➡ **Quality of Financials** – produce investor-grade financials and forecasts, normalize EBITDA, and link operations to the P&L.

- ➡ **Technology, Data, and Marketing** – move beyond spreadsheets and gut feel; use systems and data to drive growth and decisions.

- ➡ **M&A Readiness** – thoughtful approach to acquisitions, integrations, and building one company out of many.

Get these right, and you transform how an investor perceives risk, sustainability, and growth. And when perception shifts, so do multiples and deal structures.

What This Book Is—and Isn't

This isn't a pep talk. And it's not a tax manual. It's a field guide written in plain language, from inside the arena. We'll show you how to baseline your business, where to invest time and money, and when to bring in the right advisors—M&A attorneys, tax and estate planners, bankers.

We'll also tell you the truth about the emotional roller coaster: the fatigue of running a sale while running your company, the identity questions that come with letting go, and the "hangover" that often follows a deal. None of that is bad. All of it is normal. The point is to anticipate it and plan for it.

How to Use This Book

Start by getting rooted in reality. Replace your story with the investor's lens. Ask: if I got a call tomorrow, what multiple would I earn? What structure would I be offered? If you like the answer, EVRS™ will help you run a clean process and choose the right partner. If you don't, even better—EVRS™ will help you focus on the changes that matter most and give you a clear plan to execute them.

Along the way, assemble your inner circle: the right coach, deal navigator, deal attorney, tax advisor, financial advisor, and—if you run a broad process—an investment banker who can create real competition for your business. If you're married or have partners, bring them into the conversation early. Consider joining a CEO peer group. There's strength in community. And if you need us, the team at Samson is standing by to help.

We wrote this book as clearly and generously as we know how. It distills the operating system we use with founders and with investors into something you can put to work yourself. Whether you self-implement or ask for help, I hope that you walk into this process clear-eyed, grounded, and confident—not because you're guessing, but because you've designed your way there.

A Final Word

You've already done the hard part: you built a real company. Now it's time to make sure the exit—if and when you choose it—matches the caliber of what you've built. Coaches can't win the game for you. But we can help you build the system, the team, and the game plan that put you in the best position to win.

I'm grateful you've picked up this book, and I'm honored to walk alongside you as a coach in this next stage of your journey. Let's get started.

PART I: WHY?

CHAPTER 1

SELLING TO PRIVATE EQUITY

A business owner in your network, Sally, recently sold her company for a significant sum.

How did she do it? You wonder. *Could I do the same?*

At first glance, the transaction seems simple enough. A private equity (PE) firm stepped in, made a great offer, and Sally signed on the dotted line. End of story, right? But take a closer look and you'll see there's much more beneath the surface when it comes to selling to PE.

We, at Samson Partners Group, have worked with *hundreds* of private equity firms and owner-operators and have evaluated *thousands* of transactions. We understand what a well-run process looks like and have seen the pitfalls to avoid. And now we want to share that inside knowledge with you—so you can understand how private equity decision-making really works. Our goal is to help you understand how these firms think, how they evaluate businesses, and how you can best position your company if you decide to sell to PE.

Here's the great news: if you understand the dynamics of a PE transaction three to five years *before* a sale, then you can significantly increase the value of your business leading up to it. Even if you ultimately decide *not* to sell, you'll end up with a stronger, more resilient company.

This book is for owner-operators who are starting to think about *monetizing* **their businesses.**

When it comes to what you've built, you always have options. You can shut the business down. You can pass it on to the next generation in your family to run. You can sell it to your family or your employees. You can explore an ESOP. But more and more often, owner-operators today are looking at private equity as a viable—and attractive—path to a liquidity event.

Unfortunately, too many owner-operators consider preparing for a sale too late in the game. They're often disappointed with the offer and believe that the PE firms don't see the value of the business or appreciate the potential in its future growth.

The truth is, Sally, who sold her business, didn't just get *lucky*. She got prepared. And with the right insights, timeline, and execution, you can be the next owner-operator who makes the 'wow' deal with the kind of multiple everyone's talking about.

Deal Execution in Today's Environment IS NOT EASY

In the lower-middle market—companies generating under $10 million in EBITDA—the odds aren't great. Even if a private equity firm signs a letter of intent (LOI) with you, that doesn't mean that the deal will close. An LOI is just that… intent. Either party can back out of the deal at any time, and many deals fall apart during diligence. In this book, we'll help you understand *why* and the measures you can take to increase the likelihood of the transaction you want.

Let's put that into perspective. For a private equity firm to close just one deal, it may reach out to *200 companies*. Maybe 100 will engage in initial conversations. Of those, perhaps 50 will sign NDAs and share financials. From that pool, maybe three will receive LOIs. And perhaps only one of those will close.

Why? Because once a firm conducts its diligence—looking beyond your topline numbers into your leadership, culture, customer base, IT systems, operations, and risk profile—it may see issues that change the valuation OR kill the deal completely.

In this book, we want to help you understand the factors that go into diligence, how they can impact a transaction, valuation, and deal structure. If this is the path you want to go down, it is important that you step away and look at the business clinically, the way that investors will. Trust me, a firm's investment committee has no emotion when deciding to deploy capital. I want to make sure you can see your business through their eyes. If you have that courage, and the fortitude and determination to make the necessary changes, you can enhance your value at sale.

While there are countless reasons deals don't close, many of them boil down to valuation expectations and a business's actual *transactability*.

We're going to show you what *you* can control. We'll help you benchmark your company today, understand how private equity evaluates readiness and value, and map out what it would take to go from a C to an A in their eyes—so you can choose, with clarity, how to prepare and when to act.

Whether you run an HVAC business, a plumbing company, an accounting firm, a law office, a manufacturing operation, or a wholesale distribution company—it doesn't matter. Private equity knows your space. They have access to market data. They benchmark businesses like yours every day based on size, profitability, customer concentration, leadership, systems, and other operational variables.

PE valuation can be very formulaic. Numbers are plugged into a spreadsheet during due diligence. That model is going to generate a score. And just like in school, that score will be graded: **A, B, C, D, or F.**

➡ An **F** means the business is *not transactable*.

➡ A **D** means *barely* transactable—at best, the deal may get heavily restructured or repriced.

➡ A **C** may transact, but at a lower valuation and often with less favorable terms—more earnout, more contingencies.

→ A **B** is strong. It commands a better valuation and cleaner structure.

→ An **A** is exceptional. It earns a premium price and receives a streamlined process.

The trouble is, no one tells you this—not clearly, and not early enough.

Know Your Real Value

Even if you're working with an investment banker, especially in the lower-middle market, they may not have the level of insight or access to deal data that top-tier private equity and investment banking firms have. It's just the reality in this segment of the market.

Investment bankers, in many ways, are like real estate agents. Their job is to get the listing—to represent a business in a sale. And just like some realtors might overpromise to win your trust, investment bankers may tell you what you want to hear.

They'll say things like, *"Your company is worth five million dollars. I've got buyers who would love it."* But if you were to take a hard look—just as you would with a house—you might find a different story.

In real estate, we now have tools like Zillow and Redfin. These platforms have created more transparency with comps and valuations. You can instantly see how similar homes in your area sold, how long they were on the market, and what condition they were in.

If someone tells you your home is worth $400 per square foot, but the top of the market is $200 per square foot for fully renovated homes with new kitchens and roofs, then it's time for a reality check—especially if your home has a 20-year-old roof, broken toilets, overgrown grass, and a door hanging off its hinges. You might be looking at $100 per square foot, not $400 or even $200.

The same dynamic exists in the world of private business transactions. These are private markets—opaque and complex—but the truth is, private equity firms have the equivalent of "Zillow for businesses." They know the comps. They know what similar businesses in your industry, of your size and shape, are trading for. They know how long they've been on the market, what kind of offers they got, and whether or not those deals closed. You may not have the same access to this version of Zillow, but you can learn what attributes make your business more attractive to potential buyers.

Now, imagine a scenario where you *aren't* guessing what your business is worth. You're not relying on wishful thinking, or on the optimism of an eager banker trying to win your listing. Instead, you're armed with the same mindset and metrics private equity firms use to evaluate businesses every day.

You will know how PEs think. You will understand how they measure value. You will be able to benchmark your business against what the market actually rewards.

When you have reality on your side, you're not flying blind. You can look at your company with clarity—see the strengths, identify the weaknesses, and understand exactly what's creating or subtracting value. You know your score, and more importantly, you know the gap: the delta between where your business is now and where it could be if it were truly ready for a premium valuation. You see what it takes to upgrade your business.

- ➡ Maybe it's upgrading your IT systems or implementing basic cybersecurity protections.

- ➡ Maybe it's diversifying your client base so that no single customer accounts for more than 10 percent of revenue.

- ➡ Maybe it's building a sales team, so your revenue doesn't depend entirely on you, the founder.

- ➡ Maybe it's moving beyond tribal knowledge by documenting key systems and processes.

- ➡ Maybe it's replacing outdated systems, hiring a COO, or simply putting proper accrual accounting in place.

These upgrades matter. They reduce risk. They increase scalability. They make your business more attractive, your cash flows more predictable and less risky—and more valuable.

Because here's the core truth that private equity understands better than most: **the buyer is always at a disadvantage, the seller always knows more, and one thing you can never undo is paying too much.**

Buyers assess risk and return, just like lenders do with mortgages or insurers do with policies. The fewer red flags you have, the more transferable, sustainable, and valuable your business becomes.

And if there was one single metric that could sum up what buyers are looking for, it's this: the *predictability of future cash flow.*

The Predictability of Future Cash Flow

Before we close out this chapter, let's look back to the origins of private equity in the United States. The foundational insight that sparked this industry came in the 1940s, with the Pritzker family. They were among the first to pull off what we now recognize as a *leveraged buyout.*

At that time, if you wanted to borrow money to acquire a business, you typically had to back that loan with hard assets—land, buildings, equipment, or cash in the bank. The Pritzker family changed the game. They convinced a bank to lend them money based not on hard assets, but on the *future cash flows* of the business they intended to acquire. That, in essence, is the business model of private equity to this day.

When a private equity firm buys your business, it's not asking you to personally guarantee the deal with your property. What it does expect is that your business, under its new ownership, will continue to generate predictable and sustainable cash flow—*with or without you.*

That's why the structure of your revenue matters so much. A business with recurring revenue—anchored by long-term contracts, subscription models, or annuity-like services—is inherently more valuable than one built on one-off projects or unpredictable sales.

Take HVAC companies as an example. A mid-sized HVAC maintenance firm with multi-year service contracts can sell for 6 to 10 times EBITDA. By contrast, an HVAC installation contractor might only fetch 3 times EBITDA. Why? Because maintenance work provides reliable, repeatable revenue. Installation work is one-and-done and highly cyclical. If the economy slows and new construction declines, installation work dries up. But maintenance continues regardless. The systems are already installed. They still need servicing. That's *predictable*.

It's the same reason a pool maintenance company is more valuable than a pool construction company. We don't know how many new pools will be built next year. But we *do* know that chlorine still needs to be added, and filters and surfaces must be cleaned. Predictability drives the deal multiple. Or said another way, the lower the risk to the future cash flows, the higher the multiple.

If your goal is to exit the business entirely at the time of sale, that reality needs to be reflected in how your business runs long *before* the sale. You'll need to install professional management—*not right before the deal closes*, but *two to three years* in advance. You'll need to prove, with operational consistency and financial data, that the business runs well without you. If you haven't done that, the buyer may require you to stay on for a transition period—or offer less favorable terms. Because a healthy business that operates without you, the owner, is—you guessed it—more predictable.

The bottom line is this: the *type* of business you're in, the *contracts* you hold, the *customer concentration*, the *profit margins*, and the *reliance on you as the owner-operator*—all of these elements affect your valuation.

To Sell or Take on Investors? : What I Wish I Knew 10 Years Ago as an Owner-Operator

By Dave Rauch, Founder & CEO, ProTec Building Services

When you've poured decades of your life into building a business, the thought of selling it can feel impossible. You tell yourself you'll figure it out when the time comes. That's exactly what I thought—until I started buying companies myself and realized just how unprepared most owners really are.

The truth hit me hard: if I didn't start preparing early, my own company could fall into the same traps. Messy financials. Weak deal structures. Culture clashes. Botched integrations. All the things that destroy value in a transaction.

ProTec Building Services has grown to over 400 employees and 14 specialized divisions across Southern California and Nevada. We've built a predictable, recurring-revenue model serving homeowner associations. But the lessons I've learned along the way—through acquisitions we made and deals we walked away from—are the same lessons I wish I'd had a decade earlier.

Lesson One: Professionalize the Financials

When you acquire a company, one of the first things you realize is how messy small business financials can be. Too often, the seller hands you a QuickBooks export or a shoebox of receipts and calls it a day.

That's not good enough.

If you're thinking about selling your own company one day, don't wait for the buyer to tell you your numbers aren't credible. Clean them up now.

Lesson Two: Structure the Deal Wisely

One mistake I often see is sellers demanding 100 percent cash at close. It feels safer, but in reality, it's shortsighted.

The best deals are structured so that the seller keeps some *skin in the game*—through a note, rolled equity, or some other mechanism. Why? Because it aligns incentives. It creates a partnership. And it gives the buyer some downside protection.

Understand that deal structure is as important as price. A creative, balanced structure often produces a better long-term outcome for both sides.

Lesson Three: Culture Eats Numbers

Numbers can look perfect on a spreadsheet, but culture is where most acquisitions fail.

Culture is not soft stuff. It's the glue that holds the business together when everything else is in transition. Think about whether the buyer will protect the culture you've built. If the answer is no, walk away—no matter how tempting the numbers look.

Lesson Four: Integration Is the Real Work

Too many owners think the deal is the finish line. It's not. The real work starts after closing.

Integration is its own discipline: aligning systems, consolidating reporting, blending teams, and managing customer expectations. If you neglect this, all the value you thought you were buying evaporates.

Thinking About Selling

At one point, we seriously considered selling one of our divisions. We had a buyer lined up and were close to signing. We pulled out. Why? Because we didn't trust the buyer to take care of our people.

Selling is not just financial. It's personal. You carry responsibility for the employees who helped you build the business. If you don't trust the buyer to treat them well, the money isn't worth it.

What Private Equity Looks For

If you are preparing to sell to a private equity firm, know this: they're not buying your history. They're buying your potential.

Here's what they value most:

1. **Platform Potential** – Are you a business that can stand on its own and anchor a larger roll-up, or are you just a bolt-on? Platforms need systems and processes that can be replicated

2. **Professional Management** – Investors want more than loyal lieutenants. They want a trained, accountable leadership team running on a real operating system.

3. **Recurring Revenue** – Predictability is king. The more stable and sticky your contracts, the more valuable your company becomes.

4. **Cross-Sell Potential** – Can new services be layered in? Can share of wallet expand?

5. **Scalability** – Can your model work in other geographies? Scalability drives multiples.

If you want a double-digit multiple, these are the levers to pull.

The Long Game

At ProTec, we're preparing for a sale or investment around 2030. That may sound far away, but it's not. If we want to command a premium multiple, we have to do the work now.

The truth is, selling isn't just about cashing out. It's about stewardship. It's about honoring your employees, your customers, and your community. The outcome depends on how seriously you prepare.

Final Advice

Here's what I wish I had known ten years ago:

- Start preparing early.
- Professionalize your financials.
- Structure deals for alignment.
- Protect and prioritize culture.
- Treat integration as a discipline.
- Build a business that can scale, with recurring revenue and strong leadership.

And above all—stay humble. Get a coach. Learn from peers. Read. Ask questions.

Preparation is the difference between selling with regret and selling with pride.

That's the long game we're playing at ProTec. And when the right investor comes along, we'll be ready.

Private Equity Is a Relationship Business

By Ryan Sprott, Co-Founder, Great Range Capital

We meet about a thousand companies a year. That's not hyperbole. It's the reality when you're in the business of acquiring and scaling lower-middle-market, family-run companies. At Great Range Capital, we've been doing this for over 15 years. We're based in Kansas City, and we focus on first-time, Midwestern sellers—entrepreneurs or families who've never gone through a transaction. Many don't know what they don't know, and that's exactly where we come in. We take calls, we listen, and we're advisory by nature.

But that doesn't mean we'll buy every company we meet. If we speak with 100 founders who've never done a deal, we might buy one. We have to be evangelical, talking to everyone about private equity, just to get to that one. And it's not because the other 99 are bad businesses—it's because this whole process is a massive lift. A lift for them. A lift for us. And it only works when both parties are aligned.

Preparation Drives Price

Founders often underestimate how much the preparedness of their business influences valuation. The same company might be worth $100 million or $75 million depending on how much professionalization has already been done. If we have to invest in leadership, revamp financial reporting, upgrade systems, and build a strategic plan, that's cost, time, and risk. That's money off the table.

But if the seller has already tackled those things—if they've hired and mentored a successor CEO, if the financials are clean and tell the story, if the strategy is clear—then we can lean in harder. We'll pay more because the risk is lower. And we'll be eager to do so because the upside is easier to achieve.

Some owners decide it's worth it to do that work ahead of time. Others just want to be done. We're comfortable either way. But we won't pay $100 million for a $75 million business if the prep work hasn't been done.

Hiring the CEO Before You Need To

One of the most challenging situations for us is buying from an owner who also functions as the CEO—and has no one in place to take over. Let's say they want to sell and bring us in to "help find the next leader." That's a tough spot. We're buying something fragile. We do it all the time, but it's riskier than when a succession plan is already in place.

Another challenge is when an owner wants to stay on as CEO, but they just pocketed $100 million. Going forward, their motivation might not be the same. It's not that they don't care anymore. But human nature changes when you no longer need to work.

The best-case scenario is when an owner has the foresight to bring in and mentor their replacement a few years before the deal. That successor has already proven themselves. They're hungry: equity ownership provides motivation. They've been running the show: that reduces risk and increases value. And it makes the transition smoother for everyone involved.

Knowing When to Sell

When we're on the other side—looking to sell one of our portfolio companies—we ask a few questions, including: Have we hit the scale we envisioned? Have we finished the major initiatives we laid out? Are there strategic buyers circling?

In one case, we grew a landscaping company from $20 million to $100 million. We knew it could get bigger through M&A, but at the $100 million mark, the market was hot and buyers were clamoring. So we sold.

Could we have held on longer and made more? Probably. But there's always a point where holding for another two years might mean diminishing returns. That's the balancing act.

Advice for Founders

If you're thinking about selling your business, here's what I'd say:

First, get your financials in order. You don't need an audit, but you need clean, interpretable numbers that tell the story.

Second, create a basic overview of the business. Even if it's just a deck or a written summary, something that explains the company, the team, and the plan.

Third, get to know your potential buyer. This is a relationship. Fit matters. Cultural alignment matters. Trust matters.

And finally, think hard about what you want. Do you want to stay on? Step away? Run it for a while longer but take chips off the table? The more clarity you have, the better the match will be.

CHAPTER 2

WHAT IS PRIVATE EQUITY, REALLY?

Before we go any further, it's important to take a step back and define what private equity is—because there's a lot of misunderstanding out there, even among seasoned entrepreneurs.

Let's start with this: **private equity is not a mysterious, faceless force.** It's a group of folks in a structured investment model designed to (1) raise capital, (2) invest that capital in (mostly) private companies, and (3) after a holding period, return that capital and profits to the investors upon the sale of investments made. During the holding period, the invested capital is illiquid and cannot be sold or traded. This illiquidity feature means that at the first dollar of investment, private equity is already thinking about managing to its exit and its expected investor returns.

Let's go back to chapter 1's real estate analogy. Say that you and your friends pool some money to buy homes in your neighborhood, fix them up, improve them, and eventually sell them for a profit. For most of that time, your cash becomes tied up in hard assets that are not traded on an open market and are not immediately available in cash. To make a profit on your investment in these homes, you plan to make some improvements. It could be that you build an addition to the house, add a garage, or add a pool.

Each one of these improvements requires additional investment. The big idea is that investments are made for the express intent of increasing the value of the houses so that you can *sell them and make a profit*. You'll make your improvements over time–several years—and then when the market conditions are right, you'll sell to maximize your profits. In a nutshell, that's private equity.

Two Types of Private Equity Sales

When you sell to private equity, you're typically entering one of two kinds of transactions:

1. Platform Sale

This is when a private equity firm is looking to enter a new industry segment and sees *your* business as the foundational investment—what they call a **platform**. In this scenario, your company is the beachhead. You have the leadership, systems, customer base, and performance that make you the firm they want to build around. They're betting on your business to be the one they scale through organic growth and acquisition.

If you're a platform, you're the first move in a long-term strategy. You'll often remain with the company for a period of time as CEO, and the valuation and structure of the deal will reflect the strategic importance of your role.

Platform companies tend to be larger and more sophisticated. They often have stronger technology, more advanced systems and processes, and robust operational tools. They also typically feature solid leadership and low key-person risk—all of which we'll explore in detail throughout this book. Simply put, platforms tend to look quite different from add-ons, and understanding those differences will help clarify what kind of exit path your business may be best suited for.

2. Add-On Sale

The other path is being an **add-on** to an existing platform.

Let's say a private equity firm already owns a landscaping business in the Midwest. It's been looking to expand its footprint and you own a well-run business in Indianapolis. Your company becomes an add-on—a strategic acquisition that increases the existing geographic density, adds capabilities, or brings new customers under the umbrella of the portfolio company.

Add-ons are common in fragmented industries like HVAC, landscaping, accounting, and marketing services. They're still great exits—but they're valued and structured differently than platform deals, because the buyer already has leadership, systems, and strategy in place.

The Lifecycle of a Private Equity Fund

The team "Private Equity" refers to investment capital raised from institutional and high-net-worth investors pooled into a **private equity fund**. This is a professionally managed vehicle that acquires ownership stakes in private businesses, with most private equity funds having a lifespan of roughly ten years. Here's how that typically breaks down:

Years 1–3: Investment Period

The firm raises and deploys capital into a targeted number of companies (portfolio companies)—usually 4 to 6 platforms per fund, sometimes more depending on the size of the fund—and these are spaced out over the life of the fund. The first investment may take time; it's not unusual to spend a year or more sourcing and closing the initial platform deal. Companies are acquired over time, typically two to three a year. Capital is also reserved to make additional investments into the acquired companies, investing in their inherent capability and investing in add-on acquisitions to the platforms.

Years 1–10: Value-Creation Period

Once the portfolio of companies is established, the focus shifts to growth. That could mean making add-on acquisitions, expanding into new markets, implementing new systems, or upgrading the leadership team. These are the years spent actively building enterprise value. Value creation can overlap with the Investment Period and Exit Period, because value is being created all the way through the ownership period.

Years 4–10: Exit Period

The Exit Period overlaps with the value creation period (it's possible that a company acquired in year 1 is exited in year 4 or 5). In the final phase, the firm begins selling the portfolio companies, ideally at a profit. The goal is to return capital—and gains—to the investors. It is only at this point that the investment is liquidated, and cash is returned to the investors.

Unlike the public markets, where investors can buy and sell shares at any time, **private equity investment is illiquid.** The capital is locked in. No one gets paid until the portfolio companies are sold.

That's why private equity is so focused on performance. **They are working towards the exit and the liquidity event even before they start.** They can't afford to get it wrong because they must turn their illiquid assets into cash to pay out to their investors

You need to take the same approach in evaluating your business that private equity does when considering acquisitions. You should take an 'outside in' view of your company and ask yourself these questions:

1. If I were a private equity investor looking at my company today, how would I value it based on its industry, market, management team, and current infrastructure?

2. How do I compare to my peer companies?

3. What are the things I can do to the company today, and over the next 2-3 years, to improve my operations, increase its value, and make it more attractive to private equity investors?

To get the exit you want, you must first start looking at your business through the eyes of an investor. This is a critical shift when you start shaping your business toward a private equity transaction, versus shaping it to support your lifestyle, to transfer to your children, or something else.

Just like private equity, start with the end in mind (the exit you want), work back to the present, form an objective view of your company, and engineer and execute a value creation plan.

Who's Buying? The Landscape of PE Buyers

Private equity funds can be categorized by their strategies as well as by their size. Strategies can vary significantly, but they include venture capital for startups, buyout funds (which typically acquire a majority stake in companies), and growth equity (which typically takes a minority interest), to name a few. The size of the funds and the size of the acquisitions also vary greatly. We will focus our discussion on the fund types and attributes that are most relevant to owner-operators in the lower-middle market range.

We expect that most readers of this book operate businesses in the $500,000 to $10 million EBITDA range. At this level, you're primarily dealing with two or three types of private equity buyers.

Most buyers are what we call **control buyout funds**. These firms want to acquire a controlling stake in your business, typically more than 50 percent, and often 100 percent. Minority investors do exist, but they're far less common in this space.

These buyout funds can focus on certain EBITDA ranges as acquisition targets. For example:

➡ Micro-cap funds: typically target companies in the range of $500,000 to $2 million EBITDA.

➡ Lower-middle market funds: typically target companies in the $2 to $20MM EBITDA range.

- Mid-market funds: typically target companies in the $20-$60MM EBITDA range.
- Bulge bracket funds: $60MM and up, into the hundreds of millions of EBITDA.

In addition to buy-out funds, there are family offices and search funds, which compete with traditional buyout funds. Family offices operate across the spectrum of PE investing, and search funds usually compete for deals in the $500K to $15MM EBITDA range. Family offices, like buyout funds, have committed capital, while search funds do not.

Search funds aren't traditional private equity firms with committed institutional capital. Instead, they're typically individuals who want to buy and operate a single business. Business schools now teach entire courses on how to raise money and execute a search fund acquisition. The basic gist: the searcher raises a small amount of capital from a group of individual investors and/or secures a line of credit from a bank. It may have some investor backing, but the individual behind the fund is often personally guaranteeing a portion of the debt. Their model is more like a management buy-in—imagine one of your employees deciding to buy your business at a PE-style valuation by cobbling together bank financing and a few local investors. That's a search fund.

These buyers often target businesses in the $500,000 to $5 million EBITDA range, and many founders have already been approached by one or more of them. Search funds are energetic, hungry, and increasingly common. But they're also riskier because of their capital structure and often struggle to compete with the professionalism of a traditional fund.

How Are They Buying? Close Rates, Capital Risks, and the Economics Behind the Deal

In a typical private equity fund, if the firm actively evaluates 1,000 deals—meaning it's gone beyond initial conversations and has exchanged financial information—it may close about 4 to 6 platform investments over the life of a fund. That's at best a 1 percent close rate from initial review to signed deal. Along the way, the firm might issue dozens of Letters of Intent (LOIs), but not all those LOIs close.

In fact, across the board, only about **one in three LOIs from private equity firms actually closes**. Why? The reasons usually fall into three buckets:

1. **The Seller Walks Away.** Sometimes, sellers realize they're not ready. Maybe the emotional weight of selling hits them. Maybe the idea of stepping away from the businesses they've built becomes too real. One third of LOIs die because sellers pull back and decide not to go through with the transaction.

2. **The Buyer Walks Away.** Perhaps the buyer learns something during diligence that changes the story. The business may not be as advertised—maybe there are issues with customer concentration, financial reporting, leadership, or compliance. These issues often result in added risk, and the buyer walks away.

3. **The Deal Gets Recut or Stalls.** Sometimes both sides still want to transact, but the deal terms change. The valuation may be lowered, the structure adjusted, or financing may fall through. This uncertainty can stall the process indefinitely.

Now compare that to **search funds**, where only **one in nine LOIs closes**. That's a drastically lower success rate.

The reasons are somewhat similar, but amplified:

➡ Sellers may grow uncomfortable as the process unfolds, realizing that the searcher lacks institutional backing or experience.

➡ In many cases, the search funder's capital commitments aren't fully secured. Investors may back out. Bank financing may fall apart. The deal simply can't be completed.

That doesn't mean search funds can't be great buyers—many are. But as a seller, you need to understand that they're operating under a different structure, and the path to close is riskier.

You have choices. Your buyer profile matters. And your likelihood of closing depends in large part on who's on the other side of the table.

Let's return briefly to how private equity generates its returns—because understanding their incentives will help you understand how they approach your business.

Private equity firms raise capital from pension funds and other institutional investors. These investors lock up their money for say 10 or 12 years. There's no daily liquidity, no redemption. The private equity fund has to deliver results over that time period, or risk losing investor confidence—and future fundraising opportunities.

So what's the goal? Most firms in the lower-middle-market are targeting **at least a 3X MOIC—a Multiple on Invested Capital**—over the life of the fund.

In plain terms: for every $1 an investor puts into the fund, the firm aims to return $3 (or more) by the end of the holding period. That return reflects the risk taken and the illiquidity of the investment.

If the fund buys your business, holds it for a few years, and sells it, that means it needs to **rapidly grow the company's value**, either through organic growth, acquisitions, margin improvement, bottom-line delivery, or all the above. It's betting that it can scale what you've built faster and more efficiently with access to capital and expertise.

Private equity is not in the business of coasting. It's in the business of transformation. That's how it gets to its 2.5x return target—and that's why a potential PE investor looks so carefully at your business, its leadership, its systems, and its future cash flow.

What Your Deal Will Really Look Like? Cash, Rollover, and Earnouts

When it comes to selling to private equity, one of the most important concepts to understand is how **deal structure** is influenced by the perceived strengths—and risks—of your business. It's at the core of how value is ultimately realized in a transaction. Every industry in the US (and globally) has a known trade range.

CPA and accounting firms, HVAC companies, electrical contractors, plumbing companies, distribution companies, consumer product companies, veterinary companies, dental practices—every company has a known trade range. Deals are structured in different ways within those trade ranges. All owners want the highest valuation in the range and the most favorable structure. Not everyone gets there.

Here is what we always anchor to: every deal is shaped by the **predictability of future cash flows. Th e more predictable the cash flows, the higher the multiple that is applied to those cash flows to arrive at a valuation**. Based on that, along with the size of your firm, the competitiveness of your market, the shape of your revenue (recurring vs nonrecurring or project-based), the concentration of your client base the commercial terms you work within, the amount of key person risk in your business, and the strength of your leadership team, will dictate the structure and the multiple your business may be worth.

Most deals are composed of three primary components at close:

1. **Cash at Close.** This is the portion of the purchase price paid to you in cash when the transaction closes. A business with a proven track record and less risk will be purchased with more cash at closing.

2. **Rollover Equity.** This is when you, as the seller, reinvest a portion of your proceeds back into the business. Depending on the deal, you may be rolling that equity into the new platform (if you're the first acquisition in the space) or into the parent company (if you're an add-on). It gives you a second bite at the apple—but also keeps you invested in the success of the business post-close. Your rollover equity is an investment in the business going forward. *You continue to be an owner,* and the goal, along with the private equity partner, is to realize at least a 3X return on every dollar of roll-over at the end of the investment period. We refer to this as the "second bite of the apple," and for many founders this can provide as large, or larger, a return than the cash they receive at close. Our friend, Adam Coffey,

has written extensively about this in *The Private Equity Playbook*, and his books are fantastic add-ons to the learnings here.

3. **Earnout.** An earnout is a performance-based payment. It allows the buyer to tie part of the total purchase price to specific results over a defined period—usually one to three years. You might be asked to maintain revenue growth, protect margin levels, or hit EBITDA targets. If you do, you earn the remaining proceeds.

Earnouts are common when a business has had a sudden spike in performance that isn't yet backed by a long-term track record. For example, if your company suddenly grows 30 percent in a year when the historical norm is 4 percent, private equity will be cautious. That kind of growth could be an anomaly, and they won't want to pay full value for something they're not convinced will repeat.

In these cases, an earnout lets them reward you *if* that growth proves sustainable. Some earnouts are all or nothing, and some are on a sliding scale. Earnouts are a way for the investor to de-risk the investment and put accountability on the seller to continue to perform in the first few years after the initial investment. These show up a lot in times of economic uncertainty, and where businesses had a spike in growth without a long track record to demonstrate it is the new normal.

If we see founders going to market to sell a business after they have had an unusually good year—let's say historical growth was 7 percent, and they go to market after a year of growing at 50 percent—then investors will want you to put some skin in the game to prove that the growth rate is repeatable and/or that the revenue level is sustainable.

As coaches, we often advise companies wanting to avoid an earnout structure to wait another year, prove you can repeat it, and build the future backlog to prove it's sustainable. Some founders, however, may choose to ignore the advice and be ultimately disappointed at the offers they receive. A spike signals "earnout," so it's essential to understand how investors think, then make decisions and manage your expectations based on the reality of the market.

Another scenario where earnouts often show up is during **leadership transitions**. Say you're a founder with no clear successor, and you want to retire. The buyer may ask you to stay for two or three years while a new leader is groomed. During that transition, you may be asked to maintain steady performance—hit targets consistent with your historical norms.

From the buyer's perspective, this structure helps de-risk the deal. But from your perspective, it might not be ideal—especially if you were hoping to walk away cleanly at close.

That's why preparation matters.

If you want to avoid long earnouts or delayed payouts, **you need to do the de-risking before you go to market.** For example, if you know you're going to retire, install and develop your successor *now*, not after the LOI is signed. Prove that the business can operate—and thrive—without you at the helm.

Private equity is ultimately making an investment based on your future cash flows. They're underwriting risk. And how you prepare your business—how you build your team, systematize your operations, and create repeatable performance—will directly influence how your deal is structured, whether it closes, and how much money you walk away with.

In the chapters that follow, we'll break down exactly what those quality dimensions look like, and how you can start improving your position—before anyone's even signed an NDA.

Selling for Real: What I've Learned Leading and Advising Hundreds of Deals

By Christopher Geier, CEO and Managing Partner, Sikich

When I tell people I started my career in law enforcement—working tactical operations and undercover work—they're usually surprised to learn I now run a professional services firm backed by Bain Capital. Truth is, I didn't plan any of this. When I was younger, I had two goals in life: to become a professional football player or a Navy fighter pilot. I didn't have a plan C, but here I am. And as it turns out, building businesses, doing deals, and growing teams has become more rewarding than I could've imagined.

My first brush with private equity came when I was working in the sporting goods industry. The company got acquired by a PE firm, and then a couple of years later, by another.

That launched me into a 15-year run as an entrepreneur and advisor. I bought and turned around distressed businesses. I got deep into M&A advisory work.

Eventually, I joined Sikich, which was a $30 million accounting and consulting firm at the time. In 2017, I became CEO.

Since then, we've grown the firm's top line by over 300 percent, with even more growth on the bottom line. Last year, we took a minority growth investment from Bain Capital to supercharge our M&A strategy and scale in a consolidating market. That experience—as both a PE-backed CEO and as someone who's advised dozens of founder-led exits—has given me a unique vantage point.

So here's what I want to offer: practical, field-tested insight for any owner-operator thinking about a sale, especially to private equity.

Organic Growth Never Goes Out of Style

Organic growth is the most powerful kind of growth you can generate. It's cheaper. It's culturally reinforcing. And it signals something fundamental to the market: this is a team that knows how to build.

That mindset has to be part of your company's DNA. Too many businesses lean on acquisition to hit the next milestone. Acquirers see it. Private equity firms, especially, will notice if your growth engine depends entirely on M&A.

At Sikich, we have a mantra: growth without boundaries. We want our team to constantly be thinking about new opportunities—within our client base, within new sectors, through new services. A good example is our data and analytics business.

Could we have bought our way in? Sure. But M&A isn't easy. Integrations are hard. Cultures clash. And if you can grow something organically with cultural alignment and strategic clarity, you should. Acquirers value that.

You Have to Actually Want to Sell

This might sound obvious, but after doing this for decades, I can tell you: a lot of owners don't actually want to sell. They think they do. They talk like they do. They even hire an investment banker. But deep down, they haven't made the emotional commitment.

That's a problem. Because once you sign that LOI, you're in the gauntlet. Due diligence is brutal. You'll have to open up your books, your systems, your contracts. You'll be questioned. You'll be second-guessed. You'll be exhausted. If you're not 100 percent in, it will show.

Don't sign anything until you've had the hard conversation with yourself and your family. *Why are we doing this? What are we trying to achieve? Are we really ready?*

Keep Your Eye on the Ball

One of the biggest traps I see in sell-side processes is when the founder gets distracted. You've got projections. You've got earnings goals. And suddenly, you're spending all your time in data rooms and deal calls instead of running your company.

Buyers notice. And they'll penalize you if your numbers start to slip.

So my advice: perform as if the deal isn't happening. That's how you preserve value and momentum.

Clean Up Your Financials—Really

Another massive pitfall? Messy books.

This is where a lot of business owners sabotage their exit. They've been running personal expenses through the company—boats, cabins, cars, all of it. And they think a PE firm is going to give them full credit in the add-backs. They won't.

Start getting your financials in shape two to three years before you go to market. Hire a controller. Invest in better accounting systems. Get a reputable firm to help you prepare a sell-side quality of earnings report. And for the love of God, stop commingling personal stuff with business expenses.

Growth Story + Clean Books = Premium Valuation

If you want to command a premium valuation, here's what it boils down to: (1) show consistent, provable growth, and (2) make it easy for a buyer to believe your numbers.

That's it. No magic. No tricks. Just clean data and a credible trajectory.

The firms that get the best outcomes aren't necessarily the ones with the flashiest brand or biggest sales team. They're the ones that have (a) a compelling, well-articulated growth story and (b) books that hold up under serious diligence.

One More Thing: Know the Culture You're Selling Into

This last point doesn't get talked about enough. Whether you're raising capital or selling outright, you're entering into a relationship. If you choose the wrong partner, no amount of money will make it worth it.

Some PE firms are super hands-on. Others are more strategic and light-touch. Some move fast. Others are methodical. Make sure you understand not just their term sheet, but their track record. Talk to other founders they've backed. Ask what it was like year two, not just year one.

I've seen sellers get enamored with the number and blind to the dynamics. That's when regret sets in. So take your time. Ask the hard questions. And make sure the people across the table are ones you'll be proud to call partners—because after close, they are.

Closing Thought

At this point in my life, my mission is pretty simple: build great companies that help people build great careers. If we do that right, everything else—valuation, reputation, legacy—follows.

Whether you're just starting to consider a sale or you're actively preparing to go to market, my advice is the same: be honest with yourself, stay focused on performance, clean up your books, and choose your partner carefully. You only get to sell your company once—make it count.

A Sale Isn't the Finish Line

By Roy Bejarano, Founder and CEO, Scale Healthcare

Before I ever sold my own business, I spent years advising others as an investment banker. I worked in M&A at Houlihan Lokey, then ran my own boutique firm. Before that, I did time at Salomon Smith Barney in asset management. I had run deal processes. I'd pitched to private equity. I'd negotiated structures. *I thought I understood how deals really worked.*

Then I sold my own company. It wasn't theoretical anymore. It was personal.

What Most Founders Miss

Here's the part most founders don't realize until it's too late: your transaction isn't just about the money. It's about who you're selling to. Their values. Their goals. Their style.

You're not just selling your P&L. You're handing over your team. Your reputation. Your brand. You might be staying on. You might have deferred payments tied to performance. You might need to collaborate on integration.

So ask yourself: Is this someone I trust? Someone I'd work for? Would I go into business with them again?

That's how you know.

Fit > Price. Always.

If there's one message I try to hammer home, it's this: stop evaluating your sale process purely by price.

Prioritize fit. Prioritize structure. Prioritize certainty. Because the truth is, most founders are doing this for the first time—and for the last time. You can't afford to get it wrong.

The right buyer can help you clean up your business, create strategic value, and unlock long-term upside—even if the upfront check is smaller. The wrong buyer can ruin everything.

You only get one chance to sell your life's work. Make it count.

Know Yourself Before the Deal Starts

Another pattern I see: founders who don't fully understand what they're selling—or why. Is this about retirement? About risk diversification? About taking the company to the next level?

Too many sellers don't know their own goals. They just see dollar signs.

If you know what you want, you'll make better decisions. You'll negotiate for the things that matter. And you'll be more disciplined when the deal gets tough.

Advice for First-Time Sellers

If you've never sold a company before, here's my advice:

1. **Start learning early.** Selling isn't something you do once. It's something you prepare for over years. Build relationships with buyers. Learn what they value. Get your business clean and defensible.

2. **Surround yourself with pros.** Not just your cousin's lawyer or the banker with the best pitch deck. Find people who've done this dozens of times. People who'll tell you what you don't want to hear.

3. **Understand the risk.** There's no perfect deal. You'll be indemnifying, warranting, and promising things. You'll have post-close obligations. Know what those are. And negotiate them like they matter—because they do.

4. **Don't rush.** The best deals take time. Don't get swept up in the process. Control the pace. Be deliberate.

5. **Don't let price be your compass.** It's important. But it's not everything. Structure, fit, and conviction matter more.

Last Word: Be Sober, Not Swayed

Private equity isn't the enemy. I've worked with great firms. I've worked with bad ones too. There's no one-size-fits-all.

My point is this: don't get drunk on the idea of selling. Don't treat it like a lottery ticket. Treat it like the strategic, personal, high-stakes decision that it is.

Because once you're in, you're in.

And once you're out, you still might not be out—not for five years, maybe more.

So know what you're doing. Know who you're doing it with.

And if you're not sure—wait until you are.

CHAPTER 3

WHY ARE YOU SELLING? (AND, ARE YOU READY TO SELL?)

So far, we've talked about what private equity is and how deals are structured. But now, we need to talk about the most personal—and often most important—part of the equation: you.

Why are **you** considering selling **your** business?

Many valid reasons bring founders to the table. Some are strategic. Some are personal. Some are a mix of both.

Maybe you're ready to retire. You've spent years, maybe decades, investing your time, your energy, your capital, and your identity into the company. Now you want to enjoy the next chapter—travel, spend time with family, or just take a well-earned break.

Maybe you've realized how much of your personal net worth is tied up in the business, and you want to *de-risk* by taking some chips off the table. You're not done—but you want to convert some of that illiquid value into real dollars while continuing to participate in the company's upside.

Maybe you've got the entrepreneurial itch again. You built something great, but there's another venture calling to you. I've seen this happen time and again: founders who are no longer passionate about their current company because a new idea or opportunity has captured their focus.

Or maybe you're looking to expand. You want to scale, but you need capital, infrastructure, leadership, or operational support to do it. You've seen others in your industry successfully partner with private equity—either as a platform or as an add-on to a roll-up—and you want to ride that same wave. You've seen the value creation and the liquidity those founders achieved, and you want a seat at that table.

And of course, sometimes it's simply **burnout**. You've been running hard for years. You're exhausted. You've lost the passion you once had. That's okay too.

Whatever your reason, it's important to know this: **your motivation will affect how the deal is structured and whether it closes at all.**

Investors Want to Understand *Why* You're Selling

Having been on both the buying and selling sides, I can tell you that one of the first things buyers try to figure out is: *Why is this seller* really *at the table? Why are you selling now, and are you emotionally ready to sell?*

Understanding your own motivations—and being honest about them—is so important. It sets the tone for the deal. It affects how you're perceived. And it impacts your leverage and structure.

The best thing you can do as a founder considering a transaction is to be brutally honest—with yourself and with potential investors—about what's motivating you to sell. Private equity firms, especially in the lower middle market, don't expect perfection. What they do want is **clarity**.

They want to work constructively. But to do that, they need the truth—so they can evaluate whether your business fits their investment thesis and whether a deal is even worth pursuing. Remember: **to close 10 deals, a private equity firm may have to evaluate 1,000 companies**. The more transparent you are from the beginning, the faster everyone can determine if the fit is right—and avoid wasting time on both sides.

Emotional Readiness Matters

Deals don't just fall apart on financials. They may fall apart because sellers aren't emotionally prepared.

If you're joining an existing platform and haven't had a boss in 20 years, a potential buyer will want to know: Can you take coaching? Can you collaborate? Can you align with a broader strategy?

If you're becoming a platform CEO and have never worked with an investor before, are you open to feedback, can you manage change, and can you adapt to more structure, reporting, and board-level communication?

And if you're retiring, buyers want to know if you've *really* thought this through. Have you talked to your wealth manager, your estate planner, your family? Have you considered the tax implications, lifestyle changes, and what life looks like after the deal?

In short, buyers don't just want to know what you're selling. They want to know **who** they're partnering with—and whether you're prepared for what comes next.

The more prepared you are—financially, operationally, and emotionally—the stronger your position, and the better your outcome.

Is Your Business Actually *Ready* for Sale?

Once you're clear on *why* you're selling, the next big question is: *Is your business ready?*

This is where many founders get tripped up. You may have run a highly successful business for years, but that doesn't necessarily mean it's ready to stand up to private equity diligence.

Let's say you're in early conversations with a fund or even working with an investment banker. If it takes you weeks to pull together basic financials… if your accountant is still on a cash basis and can't provide GAAP statements… or if the story behind your numbers changes every time you retell it—buyers are going to take notice. And confidence will drop.

To be clear, private equity buyers don't expect every business to have an audit. That's not realistic in the lower middle market. But they do expect a level of financial sophistication that allows them to underwrite risk and make decisions. For example:

➡ If you're in construction, are you doing percentage-of-completion accounting?

➡ Are you tracking project profitability in a standardized way?

➡ Have you hired outside help to review your books and normalize earnings using accepted accounting standards?

Reliable financials and KPIs = confidence. They help justify value. They reduce perceived risk. They speed up diligence. They make a deal more likely to close—and at better terms.

Another key area? **Add-backs to EBITDA.** If your business requires tons of "normalization" to get to a different EBITDA, it may signal instability or inconsistent operations. One-time expenses are fine. But excessive or unjustified add-backs cause skepticism.

When you are ready to consider a sale (or taking on additional investors), your approach may vary based on your social and professional networks. You can do a proprietary deal with a private equity group you have come to know and trust, you can join forces with another company in your industry that has already taken on an investor and you join that platform, or you can hire an investment banker to help you get eyes on the world and meet a broader group of potential investors.

Regardless of your approach, and even if you decide not to work with an investment banker, do yourself a favor and meet with reputable investment bankers experienced in your industry. Let them evaluate your company. Let them give you comparable transactions so that you have a realistic view of price, deal structure, and timeline.

Going back to the real estate analogy: you have choices when selling your home. You can sell to someone you know, you can list the house yourself, or you can engage a real estate agent. Regardless of the option you choose, most likely you would not engage in negotiations until you've spoken with a real estate agent about the local market and/or looked at market comparables on websites like Zillow or Redfin.

Unfortunately, when it comes to sales of privately owned businesses, market comparables aren't readily available. That's why talking to an investment banker will clarify the value of your business before you engage in any serious discussions about a potential sale. It's important that you get perspectives from bankers who know and have executed transactions in your market and in your size range. Getting their insight will help manage your own expectations.

If you don't have access to credible investment bankers, leverage your network—you can find your way to them. But don't go with someone who tells you what you want to hear just to get your listing. A banker should have experience with firms like yours, with your dynamics and in your industry.

The Role of the Management Team

Equally critical—sometimes even more so—is your **management team**.

Private equity firms are *investors*, not operators. They do not want to run your business. Yes, they may get involved in strategic planning, capital allocation, M&A execution, or high-level oversight. But they're not looking to step in and manage day-to-day operations.

That means they need to believe in your leadership team.

Back in the venture capital world, we often talked about "betting on the jockey versus the horse." The jockey is the leadership team. The horse is the product, company, and market. The same principle applies here.

Private equity firms are underwriting a thesis—sure. They're betting on an industry trend, a market opportunity, a strategic roll-up. But most importantly, **they are underwriting *your* business—and *your* team.**

They want to deploy capital into strong companies with capable leaders, then stay out of the way as that capital fuels growth. Their model only works if they can trust the operators to perform. Because they're not buying a project—they're buying a performance engine.

And don't forget the math behind the model: a typical private equity fund may hold only five to ten businesses, to return **3x** capital over a 10-year period. That only works if those businesses are already strong—or at least have the leadership and infrastructure to become strong quickly.

At the end of the day, much of what drives a successful transaction—and a premium valuation—comes down to just a few key things. And it starts with **the strength of your management team**.

A capable, committed, and proven leadership team is one of the biggest value drivers in any business. If the buyer believes your team can operate the company without heavy involvement, the deal is more likely to close—and to close at a favorable valuation.

Looking at the Numbers and KPIs

Beyond leadership, there are other foundational characteristics that buyers evaluate closely:

- ➡ **Revenue Quality.** Stability and predictability of revenue are critical. Businesses with recurring/annuity-type revenue models (like subscriptions or maintenance contracts) are far more valuable than those with lumpy, project-based revenue. Predictable income means less risk—and higher multiples.

- ➡ **Customer Concentration and Payment Behavior.** If one client makes up more than 20 percent of your revenue, your business is vulnerable. That level of concentration makes investors nervous. Rule of thumb: investors want to see that the top 10 customers make up less than 20% of overall revenue. They also look closely at collections: Do your customers pay their bills on time? Do you have to chase receivables? What do your working capital and other cash flow KPIs look like?

➼ **Contracts and Pricing Power.** Too many small businesses rely on handshake deals or loosely documented agreements. Strong, well-structured contracts that **renew automatically**, **have consistently renewed**, and **include inflation-linked price increases** add real value. Even better is a demonstrated track record of taking additional pricing over time. That signals strong customer relationships and market leverage.

➼ **Process and Documentation.** If everything about your business and how it runs lives in your head, that's a problem. Buyers want **institutional knowledge**, not **tribal knowledge**. Documented, standardized processes and well-defined workflows increase confidence that the business can scale and survive leadership transitions.

➼ **Technology and Systems.** Are you still running the company off spreadsheets and patchwork software? Or have you invested in scalable, modern systems? Moving to cloud-based platforms like NetSuite or Intacct isn't just about operational efficiency—it's a signal to buyers that you've built a company that's ready to grow without breaking.

How Much of a "Lift" Will This Be? And, How Will That Affect the Deal Structure?

Another critical question buyers ask: *What kind of lift is this going to be post-close?*

If the business is heavily dependent on the founder, lacks systems, has no second-tier leadership, or requires an overhaul of financial reporting, that's a heavy lift. Buyers take that into account. It increases execution risk, slows integration, and often results in a lower offer—or heavier deal structure with less cash and more earnouts or rollover requirements.

The Seller Hangover: What Happens After the Deal

Something that doesn't get talked about enough is how to manage your expectations for both life and work when the deal is done. We call it the **seller hangover**.

Selling your business is not just a financial transaction. It's a major life event. And no matter how prepared you think you are—mentally, emotionally, or financially—it's going to take a toll.

Here's why: while you're working through the sale process, **you're still running the business**. Due diligence, negotiations, legal reviews, quality of earnings, management presentations—it all piles on top of your day job. Many founders are running at full throttle for six to nine months just to get the deal across the finish line.

Then suddenly... it's over. You've closed. The wires hit. The champagne cork pops. And something unexpected creeps in: **grief**.

You've sold your baby. You might be staying on, or you might be walking away. Either way, your identity changes. Your relationship with your business changes. The routines, the sense of control, the purpose—it all shifts.

This is normal. But it's something many founders don't prepare for, and it can catch them off guard.

Get a Plan in Place—Not Just for the Business, But for *You*

Long before the transaction closes, you need to start thinking through your **personal plan**:

➡ Have you spoken to a **wealth advisor** and **tax planner** about what this exit means?

➡ Have you mapped out your **post-close life**, especially if you're retiring?

➡ If you're staying on, do you understand what your new role looks like—and are you comfortable reporting to others after decades of running your own show?

The more clarity you have upfront, the less likely you are to feel unmoored or disappointed after the deal.

Why I Walked Away from a $500 Million Deal (and Bet on Myself for $1 Billion)

By Lauren Von Mingee, CEO, Quintessa Marketing

I didn't grow up dreaming I'd sell signed cases to personal-injury firms. That was never the plan. I stumbled into this world by solving problems one after another—and then refusing to let anyone else own the results of my work.

It started during the recession. I was in college, working the counter at AT&T, when a CEO came in to return a phone he "couldn't figure out." I sold it back to him in five minutes. He hired me as his executive assistant on the spot. I had friends with business degrees who couldn't get hired at Target; forty grand felt like a life raft.

Only later did I learn what he actually did: TV commercials for personal-injury lawyers. Ambulance chasers? That was my ignorant take. Then I sat next to the work. I picked lawyers up at the airport. I listened to what they cared about: signed cases, conversion rates, intake chaos, staffing headaches. I fetched water and took mental notes. I worked my way up and became COO.

And then I learned my first big lesson: if you don't own what you build, someone will hire a cheap guy to maintain it and thank you for your service. I left determined never to repeat that mistake.

I joined a personal-injury firm to see end-to-end: advertising, intake, case management, settlement. On my 30th birthday, at Quintessa Winery in Sonoma (yes, 9 a.m. tastings make you ambitious), I decided to start a company and name it Quintessa. The thesis was simple: run the ads ourselves, build the intake ourselves, and sell what truly matters to a personal injury firm—signed, qualified cases—on a per-sign-up basis. That was 2016.

That was 2016.

From Driver to Builder of Drivers

We didn't grow as fast as we could have at first, because I tried to be in every detail. You can't lead the same way at $5 million that you lead at $100 million. I had to shift from doing to directing; from owning every decision to building leaders who could carry the vision and execute with excellence.

So we built actual departments with real owners: Intake. Retention. Legal Marketing. Audit. Each with an executive who knows their numbers cold and a system behind them. My job became three things:

1. Set the direction.

2. Clear the path.

3. Hold everyone accountable to our values.

I can't multiply myself, but I can multiply my vision by investing in people who can scale it. That's the secret sauce.

Running It Like a Buyer Would

At some point, you stop thinking about "what pays my bills" and start thinking like a market. Investors do not want a company that depends on the founder showing up every day. They want a machine that prints results whether I'm in the building or on a beach with my kids.

We put in a full C-suite. And we track our metrics down to the penny. Financial stewardship isn't optional; it's cultural. There are only two kinds of spend at Quintessa. You either spend to generate revenue or you spend to protect revenue. Tell me which one it is and show me the ROI. If you can't, you don't spend it.

That mindset matters more as you scale. As you get bigger, it's easy for stewardship to dilute. I started this company as a single mom with no money. When you have no money, you account for every dollar. That discipline didn't change just because the top line did.

The First Dance With PE—And Why I Walked

While nine months pregnant (great timing, I know), we ran a process. The market's message was clear and useful:

➡ **Client concentration:** Too high. Diversify.

➡ **Leadership depth:** Needs to be broader than me and my husband in top roles.

➡ **Systems and scalability:** Build a leadership bench that can run without you.

We received an offer that could total around **$500 million** with an earnout. Upfront cash was more like $70–$100 million. That's real money. But read the fine print: with our leadership gaps, the earnout period would have kept me tied up for 3–5 years with a new boss on day one.

So I had a choice: bet on myself—or accept a number I knew undervalued what we could build. I'm a blackjack person. I bet on me. We've since knocked client concentration below 20%, installed a C-suite, and professionalized the business further.

Our mission is a **$1 billion** exit—and to use that event to multiply our impact through corporate responsibility and philanthropy.

The 15th Investment Banker

We interviewed fifteen investment bankers. During the interviews, I knew in five minutes who I could trust. One told me I'd never sell for $1 million. (When the big offer came in, yes, I sent a polite "update." Call it petty. I call it protective—for everyone else they might talk out of their future.)

The banker we chose was simple to describe: someone I'd grab a beer with, who didn't sell me dreams. "Here's best case, here's worst case," he said. When I paused our process with a $500 million offer on the table, he didn't punish me. He stayed in touch, invited me to meet with funds in New York, and kept building the market for the day I decided to go back out. That's a partner.

Two pieces of advice he gave me that I'll pass on:

➡ **Know your number.** Decide in advance what's "yes," what's "no," and what's "95% yes if the partner is perfect." Negotiations get spicy; you'll be tempted to take or refuse out of pride. Don't.

➡ **Make your non-negotiables list.** Like a spouse checklist for a financial marriage: integrity, goal clarity, and respect for your team.

What I Expect from a PE Partner

Right now, we're the "pretty girl on the playground." That hasn't always been the case. But at this stage, I get to be choosy—and you should too, when you've earned it.

What I want is simple:

➡ **Set the goalposts.** Tell me the return you need. If I'm hitting it, get out of the way.

➡ **Don't move the goalposts mid-game.** Ambition is great; bait-and-switch isn't.

➡ **Don't promise to "keep my people" and then quietly swap them.** We can and will upgrade where the mission requires, but trust is the only way to scale.

This is a marriage. It's a lot of money, but **at what cost?** I don't want to sell for a billion dollars and be miserable. Integrity is non-negotiable—mine and theirs.

How We're Preparing Now

We keep PE talk tight: just me and our COO are in a weekly cadence about "are we market-ready?" We don't broadcast it to the whole company. PE rumors distract; they create fear, uncertainty, and doubt. My responsibility is to keep 200 people focused on serving clients and executing the plan. When it's time, we'll tell them. Not before.

Operationally, we prepare like a buyer would:

➡ **Leadership:** Clear lanes, real owners, succession in place.

➡ **Metrics:** Every department reports a short list of KPIs that tie directly to P&L.

➡ **Cash discipline:** Dollar-level accountability; spend to make or protect revenue.

➡ **Client concentration:** No single client over 20%.

➡ **Repeatable playbooks:** Intake scripts, QA, training loops, audit rhythms.

➡ **Systems:** EOS/Traction to align vision, priorities, and accountability.

The litmus test is simple: **Can the machine print results without me?** If the answer is yes—consistently—value goes up, and deal structure gets friendlier.

Lessons I'd Hand to Any Owner Considering PE

1. **Own what you build.** Inside a company or out, structure your work so you participate in the upside you create.

2. **Replace yourself before someone else has to.** If the business relies on you, value falls, and structure gets painful.

3. **Think like a buyer early.** Not just revenue—**repeatability**. Not just profits—**predictability**.

4. **Track it to the penny.** Culture follows numbers. Dollars with a job create teams with a mission.

5. **Choose your triangle wisely.** Right banker, right buyer, right timing. You need all three.

6. **Know your number and your non-negotiables.** Decide them calm; defend them firm.

7. **Bet on yourself—responsibly.** I'm a risk-taker, but I'm a mother first. Risk should be calculated, not romantic.

Bet It All

We've built Quintessa so the result is bigger than me. That took humility (letting go) and stubbornness (never compromising the standards). Now, when we sit down with investors, I'm not selling a personality; I'm presenting a machine with values.

The market told us what would make us more valuable. We listened. We diversified. We professionalized leadership. We institutionalized stewardship. We became what a good buyer is already looking for.

When the time is right, we'll pick the partner whose integrity matches our ambition. We'll set a number and a plan. Then I'll do what I've always done: commit, execute, and hit a goal.

Until then, here's my encouragement for you if you're in that same deciding space: it's not enough to build something that pays *you*. Build something that runs **without** you. Build a team that can protect and grow it. Build the discipline that makes investors nod before you open your mouth. Then choose your moment and your partner with clear eyes.

I didn't walk away from a $500 million deal because I'm risk averse. I walked away because I'm *risk precise*. When the machine runs without me, concentration is tamed, leadership is deep, stewardship is cultural, and the partner matches our values, we'll return to market. By then, we won't negotiate from hope. We will negotiate from evidence.

I didn't pass on a payday. I chose a bigger future. Do the work that lets you walk away today, so you can walk back tomorrow on your own terms.

Going With My Gut: From Litigator to Law-Firm Buyer

By Andy Kvesic, CEO, Aprio Legal

In law school, I landed a job at a firm in Phoenix. I was twenty-something, full of piss and vinegar, and I wanted to be a litigator. I pictured myself in court, cracking heads, making arguments, being *that guy*. I started as an associate, ground it out, and made partner.

On paper, I had done everything you are supposed to do. It still felt *unfinished*.

After leaving the partnership and joining the Arizona Attorney General's Office, I became a prosecutor in the financial fraud and racketeering unit. I went on sting operations with cops. I worked with the FBI. It was the coolest job I had ever had. Then I was recruited to be general counsel at a larger state agency.

But it wasn't until I became general counsel for a family office with about forty companies on its org chart, mostly in financial services, that I learned how people with capital ***actually operate***. When to spend. When to walk. What "fit" really means. How deals die. How to keep them alive.

I thought I would do that job forever. Then a friend called with a crazy idea.

The Arizona Rule That Changed Everything

Until 2021, one rule sat like a brick on top of the legal profession across the United States: Lawyers could not share fees with non-lawyers, and law firms could not be owned by non-lawyers. The Arizona Supreme Court removed the brick. They created an Alternative Business Structure (ABS) program that allowed non-lawyers to own and invest in law firms. The aim was clear. Bring in capital. Bring in outside expertise. Promote innovation. Expand access to justice.

My buddy called, *We should buy a firm*, he said. I ignored it. He called back. We should buy this firm, *and you should run it*. He had a group of investors in mind. Pull the trigger?

I said yes.

We acquired a business law firm. I stepped in as managing partner. We had nine attorneys. We doubled our footprint. We added six or seven more lawyers and thousands of clients. The firm already handled corporate work and estate planning. That was my background. We did not chase personal injury or criminal defense. We stayed in our lane.

But it was never going to be just another firm.

A Full-Stack Professional Services Vision

Here was the thesis. Business owners do not need one advisor. They need a system. A corporate lawyer. A tax team. An accountant who can do due diligence and structure. A wealth planner. In reality, those people sit in different offices, send different bills, and speak different dialects. Even smart clients end up shuttling between professionals, trying to reconcile four versions of the truth.

I wanted to build the alternative. Make it comprehensive and make it convenient. The client never leaves.

Enter Private Equity

We did not start with an exit in mind. We were founders. Every dollar went back into the company. Better IT. Better software. Tenant improvements. Hiring. Advertising. We were not trying to polish EBITDA. We were trying to build something that worked for clients.

It was the right time. We were prepared. We closed.

What PE Looks For, What Founders Should Prepare

I had seen deals from a family office seat. I had not yet gone through a full PE transaction as a founder. Here are the lessons I learned the hard way.

1. **Tell your financial story in language investors understand.** We reinvested almost everything. I could explain every dollar. A buyer just sees thin margins. If you want a premium, prepare a version of the story that shows why yesterday's investments yield tomorrow's cash. Accrual accounting. Clean monthly closes. A bridge from controllable operational metrics to revenue and margin. A buyer will pay for durable cash flow, not vibes.

2. **Expect to be stretched.** Transactions test every muscle. Aptitude. Patience. Emotional stability. Grit. You still run the business. You still lead the team. You still go to Little League. Your clients still need their lawyer. Meanwhile, you are negotiating with bankers, investors, and your own doubts. You will feel the weight of being the founder. It is normal.

3. **"Remaining independent" is not a strategy.** Someone said that to me at the Aprio partner conference. It stuck. Independence is a state of being. Strategy is a path. If you want to stay independent, great. Define a path that wins. If you want to partner, define why. "I never want a boss" is not a plan. "I want to transform how professional services are delivered and need capital and talent to do it" is.

On the other side of our deal, here is what surprised me. The best PE partners are not breathing down your neck. They are hands-off operationally and very present strategically. They ask how to 10x in five years. They open doors. They bring discipline to the horizon. You still drive.

Why Our Deal Was a Win-Win

For our lawyers, work is steady and higher quality. We spend time on strategy, not on whether attending one more happy hour will produce a file in eighteen months. For Aprio and Charlesbank, being the first large accounting firm to integrate a law firm inside an ABS is a true differentiator. For clients, the value is obvious. One team. One plan. One bill.

For me, the personal win was less about the check and more about the weight coming off my shoulders. Founders carry a burden that is hard to describe. People have families and mortgages tied to your decisions. There are days when you wish you could be an employee again. Now I have a team behind me. Marketing. Talent. Operations. A national platform that wants us to win and will help us win.

What I Tell Founders at the Water Cooler

People pull me aside at events. They whisper *I'm thinking about PE*. Here is what I ask first.

Why now? Are you exhausted? Is it about a big check? Do you want to tell your buddies you closed with a marquee fund? Or do you see a chance to build something the market does not have yet? Be honest.

How did you get to your valuation? Be ready for a gut check. Buyers will point out the dings in your house. Do not take it personally. Treat it like inspection notes. Fix what matters. Accept what does not.

What will your business look like without you? If the answer is "smaller," you have work to do. Build a team. Build systems. Build demand that does not depend on your personal oxygen.

What do you want your life to look like after the deal? If the idea of reporting to a board makes you itch, say so. If you want to sprint, say so. If you want to be Mr. Inside or Ms. Outside, say so. Clarity is a gift to everyone.

PART II: WHEN?

CHAPTER 4

THE THREE-YEAR PLAN

Recently, I sat down with a founder of a personal injury law firm. He said, *"Seth, I want to sell my firm and walk away in three years."*

And I told him the truth: *"If that's your objective, we need to start now."*

Here's the reality. His name is on the building. His name is on the billboards. His name is on every piece of advertising. He's still trying cases. He's still managing the team. The entire business is dependent on him.

So why would an investor pay a premium—*and* **let him walk away?** What is the buyer paying for? The business might not survive the founder's departure. And if there's uncertainty about future cash flow, the valuation goes down—or the deal won't close at all.

The solution? It's not simply putting someone in a leadership seat with the CEO title the month before you go to market. That's not a transition— that's a stunt. Private equity firms will see right through it.

If you want to step away from your business and achieve a clean exit, you need to engineer a real leadership handoff. That means identifying, grooming, and installing someone into the operational leadership of the company *at least* two years before your planned exit.

Here's what that looks like in practice:

➡ You bring in a professional leader—whether internal or external.

➡ You gradually shift decision-making responsibility.

➡ You stop running the day-to-day.

➡ You give that leader room to lead.

➡ You stop showing up to the office as the de facto authority.

➡ You rewire the culture so that leadership, clients, and staff align with the new team.

Then, you let that new structure *prove itself.* Not just in conversation, but in performance that's visible in the numbers.

When the time comes for diligence, private equity firms will do more than read organization charts. They'll check keycard logs. They'll conduct employee interviews. They'll review communication patterns. They will gain a deep understanding of how you win and service work. And they'll quickly learn whether your firm is truly independent of you—or whether you're still the hub of the wheel.

What happens if you get this right? You create a business that is no longer founder-dependent. And that unlocks exit options. It gives buyers confidence. It increases valuation. And it allows you to walk away with both a successful deal *and* your legacy intact.

Many owner-operators are, quite frankly, the entire show. They're the face, the engine, and the safety net of the company. That's not inherently a bad thing. In fact, it's often what made the business successful in the first place.

But if your goal is to sell the business and walk away at the time of the transaction, here's the truth: **that's not going to happen**—not unless you've taken proactive steps to make the business independent of you.

Some founders actually *do* want to stay. They want to continue running the business, take on the role of platform CEO, and participate in the next phase of growth under new ownership. They want a second bite at the apple—or a third. My friend Adam Coffey talks about this in his writing: "Don't sell your business once. Sell it three times." That's the private equity playbook. Roll over equity, partner with the firm, grow it again, and go through another sale.

And if that's your goal? Fantastic. Let's help you maximize value along that journey too.

Regardless of your exit strategy, the same fundamentals apply. It's those we've mapped out in our Exit Value Realization System (EVRS)™:

➡ **Vision and Strategy** – not just where you've been, but where an investor can take the business next.

➡ **Human Capital and Leadership** – reduce dependency on the founder, build a second line, and show the company runs without you.

➡ **Quality of Revenue and Growth** – diversify customers, build recurring revenue, create pricing power, and professionalize sales.

➡ **Quality of Operations** – document processes, measure results, expand margins, and make the machine run tighter.

➡ **Quality of Financials** – produce investor-grade financials and forecasts, normalize EBITDA, and link operations to the P&L.

➡ **Technology, Data, and Marketing** – move beyond spreadsheets and gut feel; use systems and data to drive growth and decisions.

➡ **M&A Readiness** – thoughtful approach to acquisitions, integrations, and building one company out of many.

What is a potential buyer evaluating when they ask these questions? Do the numbers reflect the state of your business? What are your cash flows and are they predictable, reliable and sustainable post-close? Preparing to sell to private equity is a sound business strategy because even if you don't, the business will be stronger for the effort you've put in to clearly answer these questions and make your business valuable.

How Strong Is Your Business?

We stress *anti-fragility*. A fragile business breaks under stress. An anti-fragile business absorbs pressure, adapts, and gets stronger.

Let's look at this in practical terms.

If one of your customers accounts for 60 percent of your revenue, your business is fragile. Lose that one account, and you might have to lay off employees or scale down operations. Compare that to a business where the top 10 customers make up just 20 percent of total revenue. Losing one client might sting—but it won't crater the business. That's a less fragile business. That's a business built to withstand disruption.

Now take leadership. Imagine you're the founder, and most of the revenue flows from your personal relationships. You lead sales. You're the face of the brand. You make the deals happen. You employ 30 people—but if something happens to you, the whole thing grinds to a halt.

Now let's play it out.

Maybe you win the lottery and disappear to the south of France. Or maybe something more serious happens—an illness, a family emergency, a burnout that forces you to step away.

In either case, the business suffers. Your employees are at risk. Not because they didn't work hard. But because *you* didn't make the business resilient. You didn't build systems or delegate authority. It all depended on you.

Now, picture this from the perspective of a future buyer. You're asking someone to invest millions of dollars into your company. It's going to evaluate one thing above all else: **how anti-fragile is this business?**

That's just another way of saying: **how predictable are the future cash flows?**

➡ Is the business over-reliant on a few accounts?

➡ Do clients stay and spend more, or do they churn?

➡ What happens now that you've walked away?

- Are you running on modern, secure, scalable systems, or is your infrastructure duct-taped together with outdated software (or no software) and tribal knowledge?

I've seen companies still running on spreadsheets—no cloud backup, no centralized data, no operational consistency. That's fragility.

Compare that to a business running on NetSuite or Intacct. Systems are cloud-based. Financials are accessible in real-time. Documentation is standardized. Knowledge isn't locked in someone's head or on a single hard drive. That's anti-fragility. That's scalability.

And regardless of whether you're selling, that's smart business.

But if you *are* selling—or even thinking about it—you need to start viewing your company the way potential outside investors would. Their mindset is: **Will this business hold up over time? Can it grow under pressure? Or is it one misstep away from falling apart?**

Executing the Three-Year Plan

When private equity values a business, it's primarily focused on one thing: **The strength and predictability of future free cash flows.** Your three-year plan should be focused on building that predictability.

But what drives that predictability? It comes down to **six core factors**—each of which directly influences valuation and deal structure:

1. **Quality of EBITDA.** Are your earnings before interest, taxes, depreciation, and amortization strong, consistent, and truly reflective of the underlying business performance? Have they been properly normalized and adjusted in a way that a buyer would trust?
2. **Quality of Earnings & Revenue.** Is your revenue recurring or project-based? Are your earnings sustainable, or are they inflated with one-time events, personal expenses, or aggressive accounting? Investors want clean, repeatable, verifiable numbers that can withstand diligence.

3. **Quality of Leadership.** Can your business run without you? Have you developed a leadership team that can scale, make decisions, and perform in a post-transaction environment? Private equity doesn't just invest in a founder—it invests in a system led by capable people.

4. **Quality of Operations.** Are your systems, processes, and delivery methods consistent, efficient, and scalable? Do you deliver strong outcomes for customers with predictable margins and performance? Operational excellence is what allows growth to happen without chaos.

5. **Quality of Finance and Accounting.** Are your books clean, current, and investor-grade? Can you close the month, forecast accurately, and tie operations to the P&L? High-quality financials inspire confidence and directly impact both valuation and deal structure.

6. **Quality of Growth.** Is your business positioned for sustainable expansion—organically or through acquisition? Do you have a credible plan to capture market share, deepen relationships, and expand margins? Growth quality determines whether a buyer sees your company as a platform or just an add-on.

These six areas drive valuation—and each one is within your control. They can't be perfected overnight, but in three to five years, they can be strengthened to a level that transforms how investors perceive your business.

Over the next **six chapters**, we'll walk through how to assess, strengthen, and demonstrate these **six core qualities** that determine your company's value in the eyes of private equity.

Preparing for What's Next, Without Rushing It

By Brick Thompson, Co-Founder of Data & Analytics Firm, Blue Margin Inc.

Fourteen years ago, my brother and I founded our company with a simple goal: build something we'd actually want to work at. We weren't chasing a flashy exit. We weren't trying to ride a wave of investor capital. We just wanted to create a high-integrity business that delivered real value, treated people well, and gave us the freedom to make long-term decisions.

We've stayed true to that. We never took venture money. We didn't borrow a dime. We've been profitable every year since we started, even through some hard ones, including the two-and-a-half years post-COVID, when everything felt like walking through molasses. And now, with a team of about 40 people, mostly based in Fort Collins, Colorado, we're back on a solid growth trajectory.

These days, we're starting to think more seriously about a future transaction. Not because we're in a rush, but because we want to be ready. This isn't my first rodeo with private equity. In my prior life, I started a telecom data company that we sold to private equity as part of a roll-up.

Building Without the Pressure

When my brother and I began, we knew we didn't want to answer to a Board. We didn't want the pressure of financial metrics driving every decision. That's not to say we didn't care about profitability. We've always run lean and focused. But we were building a company we liked, not just a company someone else would want to buy.

That freedom came with trade-offs. Growth was slower, and at times, we had to wait to hire the talent we knew we needed. But over time, we've grown into a solid, mid-market data and analytics company. We work with PE-owned portfolio companies all the time. Our tools help them with business intelligence, reporting, and data strategy. So even though we haven't sold to PE ourselves (yet), I've seen plenty of these transactions play out.

Watching the Play from the Sidelines

Because we work with so many PE-backed companies, I've had a front-row seat to how private equity operates. Some of our best customer relationships came from PE operating partners referring us into their portfolios. And it's clear: the PE industry has gotten very good at this.

They're n ot s praying i nvestments l ike v enture c apital fi rms. The y're precise. They're methodical. Th ey know what they're looking for—companies with strong profitability, stable growth, and a clear opportunity to scale or roll up. They're underwriting the business, not just betting on potential. And when they commit, they expect results.

That level of rigor changes everything. When you're PE-backed, you've got reporting requirements. You've got board meetings. You've got an exit horizon. During my first PE experience, I spent 30–50 percent of my time just managing the board.

That's not inherently bad, but it's a shift. You're no longer just running the business: you're running the board's expectations, too.

Don't Wing It

Today, we're getting inbound interest at least weekly. Some firms are doing research. Some are scouting. Some are rolling up a thesis in our space. We're not biting yet—not because we're uninterested, but because we're being deliberate.

There's a lot that gives us confidence. Our revenue growth is steady and accelerating. Our profitability is solid. Our sector, data and analytics, isn't going anywhere. If anything, AI and digital transformation are making it more essential. We're also making smart hires and investing in our leadership team. And while I'm 61, I'm not slowing down. I could easily work another ten years if the work stays interesting.

But when the time comes, I don't want to wing it.

We're already thinking about succession planning. We've mapped out key roles that will need to be filled. These are positions we didn't need or couldn't afford a few years ago but will need if we want a premium valuation. That includes commercial leadership, finance, and operations.

We're not waiting until the last 12 months to figure that out.

What a Good Exit Might Look Like

Ideally, we'd sell to a strategic buyer—someone who really gets what we do and sees how we make them better. Maybe we'd carry equity into the next phase. Maybe there'd be an earnout. We're open. We could also sell to PE, as a platform or as an add-on. We don't have a fixed outcome in mind. But we want options—and leverage. And that means preparing now.

We've also seen some cautionary tales. Founder fatigue is real. I've watched people sell, retire early, and then get bored. They build the dream house. They realize they're not going to get better at golf. Then they call me six months later, asking if I've heard about anything interesting they can jump into.

Others have great outcomes but burn out trying to manage the board or force a fit with a partner they don't align with. One friend thought he'd stay on for three years. He was gone in three months.

You can't control everything, but you can set yourself up to have choices.

No Rush, Just Intentionality

We're not chasing the shiny object. We're not racing toward a finish line. But we're moving with intention. We're mapping our talent strategy, clarifying our growth thesis, and understanding what a buyer will care about. And when we get there, whether it's a strategic buyer or a PE firm, we want to be ready.

Until then, we'll keep building the company we love. And doing it in a way that ensures someone else will love it too, when the time is right.

Building a Billion-Dollar Roll-Up: What I've Learned About Private Equity, Partnership, and the Long Game

By Steve Carroll, CEO & Co-founder, Kelso Industries

When my childhood friend and I set out to buy a business together, we had no idea we'd end up leading a billion-dollar PE-backed platform with more than 150 employee-owners and 26 acquisitions under our belt. We just knew we wanted to build something — together — and we thought maybe a small business acquisition would be a good place to start.

I'm Steve Carroll, co-founder of Kelso Industries, named after the elementary school where my business partner and I met in the fourth grade. Our story is a little different from the typical founder-to-sale arc. We weren't looking to sell a business to private equity: we were looking to build one with private equity. And what we've learned over the past several years could help others who are trying to figure out where they fit in this growing ecosystem of capital, consolidation, and change.

We Didn't Plan for PE—We Needed It

Originally, we thought we'd just get an SBA loan, buy a business, and run it ourselves. My partner had a background in private equity and investment banking. I came up through the trades and later had a corporate career at Walmart. We figured we had a good balance of skills.

But the business we started needed more capital than the SBA could provide. Between the purchase price and the working capital requirements, we were looking at an $8 million need. That was our first wake-up call: banks aren't as willing to support low-asset, service-based businesses the way they used to. We had trucks and leases and a lot of employees, but not the kind of fixed assets lenders love.

Private equity stepped in to fill the gap.

We partnered with Peterson Partners, a Salt Lake City-based firm where I happened to know one of the partners from my MBA program. That relationship, and the years of mutual respect between my business partner and him, made all the difference. We didn't just get capital. We got a partner who believed in the vision and backed us to pursue it.

From $2 Million to $100 Million EBITDA

Since then, we've grown from $2 million in EBITDA to over $100 million. We've acquired 26 companies. And we've done it in a way that emphasizes partnership—not just with our PE sponsor, but with the owner-operators who've joined Kelso through acquisition.

Our approach is different from what a lot of people expect when they hear "private equity." We don't throw out the playbook or gut the company. In fact, we never offer the highest price. We tell sellers upfront: "If you're just looking for the biggest number, we're not your buyer. But if you want a partnership, we might be the right fit."

That's not just a line, it's a philosophy.

Succession Is a Years-Long Process

One of the most important lessons we learned came from our very first acquisition. It was a husband-and-wife team—he ran the operations, she handled the finances — and they both exited just two weeks after closing.

That didn't work.

We thought we could just step in and take the reins, but we underestimated how much of the company's DNA was wrapped up in the founder. The customer relationships, the team culture, the way decisions got made—we were walking into a hornet's nest.

From that point forward, we began to rethink how we approach succession.

Now, when we buy a company, we look for alignment. Financial alignment. Cultural alignment. Leadership alignment. Most of our sellers roll over 5% to 30% of the proceeds into equity in Kelso. That means they stay involved, they stay motivated, and they share in the upside. And we think of succession as something that plays out over years, not months.

Relationships Are Everything

In our case, relationships have made all the difference.

My co-founder had known our initial PE partner for over a decade. They'd never done a deal together, but they'd built a lot of trust over the years. That made a huge difference when it came time to negotiate, close, and build something together.

I tell owners all the time: don't get distracted by the big number on the LOI. That's just a headline. What matters is the relationship behind it. Who are you going to be in business with? What happens if things go sideways? Can you have hard conversations? Will they still have your back when the market turns?

That's why reference checks matter. Talk to other founders who've worked with the firm. Ask about exits, about how they handled conflict, about how they delivered on their promises. A good PE relationship is a long-term one. If you can't see yourself partnering with them for the next five years, keep looking.

The Soft Side of the Deal Is the Hardest Part

When people talk about M&A, they tend to focus on numbers—valuations, multiples, earnouts, rollovers.

But what makes a deal succeed or fail often comes down to the soft stuff. Emotions. Trust. Identity. The founder's sense of purpose after the sale. The team's morale. The fear of change.

That's where people like Seth come in. He's been on both sides of these deals, and he knows how to navigate the emotional terrain. The spreadsheets don't tell you how it feels to hand over your life's work. They don't tell you what to do when a founder's losing sleep because he's not sure he made the right call. But Seth can help with that. And that's why his perspective is so valuable.

Final Thought

If you're a founder thinking about selling, my biggest advice is this: don't sell just because you're tired. Don't sell just because the number looks good. Sell when you know *who* you're selling to—and why.

Find the partner who shares your vision and your values. Make sure there's alignment—not just financial, but operational and cultural. And if you're going to roll equity, make sure you believe in what you're rolling into.

At Kelso, we didn't start out thinking we'd become a billion-dollar company. We just wanted to build something great. With the right partners and the right values, that's exactly what we've done.

And we're just getting started.

PART III: HOW?

CHAPTER 5

QUALITY OF EBITDA

We often talk about cash flow as the "North Star." Predictable, sustainable, and growing cash flows are what drive value. But when it comes time to calculating those cash flows (to ultimately determine how much a company may be *worth*), nearly every private equity investor starts with the same measure of cash flow: EBITDA (earnings before interest, taxes, depreciation, and amortization).

Most business owners may be used to thinking in terms of net income, taxable income, or cash in the bank. But when private equity firms evaluate your company, they start by reviewing your financial information prepared in accordance with GAAP (not tax basis). Those GAAP (Generally Accepted Accounting Principles) earnings are used to compute a "normalized' EBITDA.

Normalized EBITDA represents an apples-to-apples measure that allows potential investors to evaluate the trendline of your business over several years and also allows investors to more easily compare one company to another. It's your ongoing, recurring cash flows, stripped for nonrecurring and unusual items (may be either additions to or deductions from the metric, depending on the nature of the items).

Did you run a family vehicle through the business? That gets added back. Did you pay yourself an above- or below-market salary? That gets normalized (added back or deducted depending on whether you paid yourself above or below market). Did you incur a one-time cost to implement a new ERP system? That gets added back. Did you receive a large insurance proceed from a claim? That gets deducted.

It's the normalized or adjusted EBITDA that investors really care about. It's this number that lenders use to underwrite debt. It's the measure investors use to assess returns. It's what drives valuation.

The valuation of your business is ultimately determined by multiplying your normalized EBITDA by a factor or a multiple. You may hear investors say that a business is worth 6X. The 'X' represents normalized EBITDA, and 6 is the multiple the investor is applying to arrive at a valuation and a likely purchase price. That multiple becomes the multiplier on your earnings that drives enterprise value.

Private equity firms have data banks of past transactions that cover a range of industries and companies of varying sizes within each industry. When buyers are evaluating your business, they are typically considering a range of multiples to apply to your normalized EBITDA. The quality of your EBITDA will determine whether you are at the low end or the high end of the multiple range (specific for your size and industry).

How sustainable is your cash flow? How diversified are your customers? How professionalized is your team? How defensible is your market position? How will the business perform without you? During due diligence, potential investors are not just looking at the current year performance of your business, but they are risk-assessing the predictability of those cash flows into the future. Their risk assessment determines whether a low multiple or a high multiple is applied to your normalized EBITDA.

Private equity firms know these ranges. Good investment bankers know them, too. But founders often don't. Instead, they hear a story from someone who sold for a big number and assume the same logic applies to their business—without context. Maybe it does. Maybe it doesn't. The key is to understand where your business *actually* stands.

Let's recap: every industry has trade multiples, and these multiples move over time. You need to speak with investment bankers in your industry to understand the current comparables for your business. Based on all the factors we have discussed, your business has an expected value. Based on a realistic assessment of your business, you can seek a liquidity event now, as is, or shape the business to achieve a higher valuation, which will take time.

Whichever path you choose, take time to truly understand the market and make decisions based on the type of exit you want. It is critical to be grounded in reality and by evaluating and valuing your business the same way private equity would, from the outside-investor-view-in.

Where Do You Land?

Your industry has a benchmark range. You're somewhere in it. And that means you have a choice.

If you're thinking about selling—especially in the next three to five years—you can start making decisions now that improve your adjusted EBITDA, improve your quality score, and command a higher multiple when you do go to market.

That's the essence of the three-year plan.

Understand how investors view your business. Benchmark yourself honestly. And then choose whether or not to invest in closing the value gap.

Earning Your Valuation: Insights from an Investment Banker

By Quinn Carlson, Uplift Partners

Selling your business isn't flipping a switch. It's more like prepping for a heavyweight title fight: if you want to come out on top, you better be in fighting shape. I've been an investment banker for over a decade, advising owner-operators on their exits—some of them five years in the making. I speak plainly to clients in your position: if you're aiming for a premium valuation and a clean exit, **there's a right way to prepare and a wrong time to rush.**

The Path to Maximum Valuation Runs Through the Management Team

Let's get one thing straight: you won't get top dollar if you're still running the business day-to-day. If you're the key person holding everything together, you're not selling a business—you're selling a job. And buyers aren't interested in paying what they view as a premium for a business that they need to find a new CEO to run. They're looking for a machine that runs on its own.

To truly exit, you need a leadership team—especially a CEO or President—who has been in the seat long enough to show results. That means at least a year, ideally more. Buyers will want to see if performance improved, stayed consistent, or faltered without you at the helm. That's their way of pressure-testing whether the company can thrive without you.

I'll say this plainly: if you don't have a strong second-in-command (and no, not a family member), you're not ready to sell.

CFO Readiness Is a Deal-Breaker

Here's another deal killer: financials that take 45 days to close. If you can't tell me how your business did last month by the 7th of this month, that's a major red flag. PE firms expect speed and accuracy. If they have to wait for basic financial info—or if numbers don't tie out to tax returns—you'll lose their interest fast. At best, you'll be viewed as an "operational improvement story." At worst, they'll walk away.

A good CFO is non-negotiable. If you don't have one, get one—well before you go to market. Think of it this way: when a buyer sends a letter of intent (LOI), the next 90 to 120 days are like a stress test. Your CFO will be working overtime to fulfill diligence requests while keeping the business on track. If you're missing that function, you might not survive diligence intact.

Growth, Margins, and Management: The Valuation Trinity

When investors look at your company, they're really evaluating three things:

1. **Growth** – Are you outpacing your market? Is there a credible growth story?

2. **Margins** – Are they strong and stable? High-margin businesses get higher multiples.

3. **Management** – Can your team run the company without you? Do they have a vision?

Of those three, management is the hardest to quantify—but the most important. You know it when you see it: a team that's hungry, professional, and aligned. If your team shows up to a management presentation unprepared, uncertain, or unable to explain your market strategy, you can kiss a premium valuation goodbye.

Show the Vision or Lose the Deal

Here's a test: imagine a buyer gives you $5 million to grow your company. What do you do with it?

If you don't have a confident, detailed answer, you're not ready to sell. It's not enough to say "we want to grow." Buyers want to see a real plan—acquisitions, new regions, new verticals, capacity expansion, pricing levers. Whatever the angle is, someone on your team needs to own that story.

And no, you can't fake it. PE firms are sharp. If you try to bluff your way through, they'll see it a mile away.

The founders who do best are the ones who say, "Here's the opportunity, I've carried the ball this far, and now I'm ready to bring in a partner to help take it further." That's a compelling message.

Asking the Right Questions

You don't need to wait until you're ready to go to market to call a banker. In fact, the best results often come from relationships that start two or even five years before a deal. I'm working with a client now—a $100 million dental business we've been advising pro bono for five years. No pitch deck, no teaser, no fee agreement. Just thoughtful preparation.

Founders often ask, "What's my business worth?" But that's not the right question. The better questions are:

➡ "What comps should we be compared to?"

➡ "Should we trade at a premium or a discount to those comps?"

➡ "Who would buy us—and why?"

➡ "What do I need to fix to get a better multiple?"

Those questions tell me you're serious. They tell me you want to do it right.

Avoiding the Parade of Nonsense

When founders put out an open call to investment banks, what they usually get is what I call the "parade of nonsense." Every banker shows up with a slick pitch deck and says almost the exact same things along these lines:

➡ "You're valuation is between X and Y."

➡ "Now is a great time to exit."

➡ "We love your business" and/or "The market will love your business."

➡ "We know the entire buyer universe."

But what matters, assuming you are ready, isn't the pitch where you hear everything that makes you feel good—it's the process of the sale. Only through a really strong, well-run process can you then answer the really important questions: "What does a good deal look like? What does a great deal look like? What story resonates with which buyers? What doesn't resonate, and will someone tell me these hard truths?"

You don't need a cheerleader. You need a coach who's willing to bench a player, call a timeout, and run the play that wins.

When We Say "No"

We don't take every deal. If a company is too small—under $10 million in revenue—and not very profitable, it's probably not going to attract buyer interest. If the books don't reconcile, if revenue recognition is all wrong, if there's high turnover or unresolved employee issues, we'll politely pass.

It's not personal. It's about readiness.

Diligence today is brutal—up to 12 workstreams, often over 90–120 days. If we don't think a company can hold up under scrutiny, it's better not to go to market at all. A busted process is painful and hard to recover from. Once a deal falls apart in diligence, it taints the business. Other buyers assume something was wrong—and they'll lower their offers accordingly.

Your Job During the Deal: Overperform

Here's something most sellers underestimate: once you go to market, you're working two jobs. You're still running the company, but now you're also selling it. Diligence doesn't pause because you're busy. Lawyers will haggle over reps and warranties while buyers demand updated financials every month.

The last thing you can afford during this time is a dip in performance. You need to meet—and ideally exceed—your projections. Buyers want momentum. If your numbers start to slide, they'll get cold feet or revise terms downward.

You can't just "do okay." You need to overperform.

When It Goes Right

When it all comes together—when the company is prepared, the leadership team is strong, the financials are tight, and the growth story is compelling—we can light up the market. On our last deal, we generated over 50 proposals. That's not a typo. Fifty.

And among those proposals, we got outliers. Buyers who just had to have the business. That's how you get premium valuation—not just a good multiple, but great terms: more cash at close, less structure, cleaner agreements.

We've invested heavily in processes that help us move fast, keep diligence tight, and bring in as many buyers as possible. That's how you create competition, and competition drives price.

If you're reading this and thinking, "That's not where I am yet," that's okay. That's the point. Start early. Ask the right questions. Build the team. Shore up your financials. Lay out the growth plan. And pick the right advisor—not the one who flatters you, but the one who prepares you.

Selling your business is the biggest financial decision of your life. Treat it that way.

The Buy-Side: What Buyers See That Sellers Miss

By David Harvey, Founder and CEO, Harvey and Company

I run a buy-side firm, which means we work for buyers, not sellers. Most advisors in M&A run processes for owners who want to sell. We do the opposite. Our clients are private equity funds and their portfolio companies that want to acquire founder-led and family-owned businesses in privately negotiated, non-auction situations.

That vantage point matters. I live in the pattern recognition of the buy side. Over twenty-seven years, Harvey & Company has closed more than 1,100 buy-side transactions, including 600 in the last four years alone. We have 130 professionals organized by industry. In 2024, by the number of deals closed, we were the third most active M&A advisor in North America. I share that only to make one point. I sit across from a lot of owner-operators, and I watch many of them get the outcome they hoped for while others fall short. From my chair, the difference is not luck. It is preparation and a clear understanding of how buyers think.

Platform vs. add-on: how buyers decide

Private equity builds value in two main ways. They improve operations, and they compound through acquisitions. To compound, they need a **platform** that can absorb other businesses. That platform can be your company, or your company can be an **add-on** to someone else's platform.

What makes a platform:

➟ A management team that can run the business without the founder in every room

➟ Financial reporting that closes cleanly and tells the truth

➟ Operating systems and IT that can integrate acquisitions

➡ Enough scale to support the overhead that true professionalization requires

You do not need to be big to be a platform. More funds are starting with smaller businesses than ever before. But if a company lacks the team, processes, and systems to be the center of a buy-and-build strategy, a buyer will either pass or treat it as an add-on. That can still be a great outcome. Just understand the role you are signing up for and price it accordingly.

There is a third path that many founders overlook. If you are close to being a platform, you can **invest ahead** of a transaction. Upgrade the finance function. Put in the IT stack. Hire the COO or president who makes you less essential. Your margins may dip for a year. Your value will often increase far more than the hit to EBITDA.

A Quick Story: From Tiny to Platform to Exit

A few years back, we helped a fund buy a small third-party administrator that processed health claims for self-insured employer plans. It was a tiny initial investment. Good core business. Not yet a platform.

The fund did three things.

1. **Upgraded the people.** They brought in a stronger leadership bench while keeping the founder in a role that matched his strengths.

2. **Built the infrastructure.** They invested heavily in the claims platform and the analytics behind it.

3. **Executed a buy-and-build.** A handful of follow-on acquisitions added geography, capabilities, and scale.

Four years later, the fund sold a company that looked nothing like the one we helped them buy. Measured on a price-per-share basis for the founder's rollover equity, it was a 5.5x outcome. He never would have captured that upside without the initial deal and the work that followed.

Two takeaways. First, small can become a platform if you commit to systems and leadership. Second, rollover equity can be very powerful when paired with a credible buy-and-build plan.

What Pushes Multiples Up or Down

Multiples move with four factors:

1. **Growth rate.** Faster growth attracts more buyers and better terms.

2. **Margins.** Strong, defensible margins imply pricing power and operational discipline.

3. **Recurring revenue.** Contracted, subscription, or behaviorally sticky revenue is valued higher than one-time or lumpy work.

4. **Risk.** Customer, supplier, product, and key-person concentration all depress value.

If revenue is recurring and churn is low, buyers may lean on a revenue multiple. If revenue is project-driven and volatile, the market leans harder on EBITDA and discounts variability. A company that is bigger, growing faster, safer, and easier to underwrite will always command a better price and cleaner structure.

One more driver that many owners miss. Buyers love **roadmaps.** If there is a credible role-model company that shows the playbook works, valuation lifts. If you have already executed small acquisitions or have a pipeline of targets you can articulate, that also lifts value. Private equity is increasingly building portfolios around acquisitive companies because the arbitrage is real. You can benefit from that long before you sell if you demonstrate the same capability.

Why Deals Fall Apart

We win a lot, but we still lose more than we win. The number one reason deals fall apart is simple. **The company misses its numbers during the process.**

Two common causes:

➦ **Distraction.** The sale process soaks up leadership time. New business development and operational focus suffer. Results dip at the worst possible moment.

➦ **Over-promising.** The forecast the seller shows on day one is closer to hope than plan. When actuals fall short during exclusivity, buyers retrade or walk.

The cure is boring and effective. Understate a bit. Deliver a lot. During a process, it is far better to say "we over-performed" in the eleventh hour than to explain a miss. Build a deal team that shields the operating team so the business keeps humming.

How to Raise Your Valuation in the Next 12 to 36 Months

If you plan to exit or partner with private equity soon, stack the deck now. Here is the short list that moves the needle most.

Hire a killer CFO.

You do not need a Fortune 500 veteran. You do need a leader who closes on time, runs accrual accounting, builds a budget you can hit, and produces dashboards buyers trust.

Upgrade systems.

Put in IT and financial systems that scale and speak the language of lenders and buyers. Clean general ledger, CRM that tracks pipeline and conversion, and an ERP that can integrate add-ons. Good systems make diligence short and valuations strong.

Reduce dependency on you.

The most common red flag we see is a business that is the owner. Build a team that runs sales, operations, and finance without you. If you can take a two-week vacation and nothing changes, you have just raised your multiple.

De-risk concentration.

No single customer above 15 percent, if you can help it. No single supplier you cannot replace. No single product or service that carries the entire P&L. The more you diversify, the more buyers you attract.

Keep upgrading talent.

Longevity is wonderful. A closed talent market is not. Keep bringing in new athletes. The CFO you could afford at ten million will not be the CFO you need at fifty.

Consider investing ahead of the deal.

Yes, expenses may rise. Yes, EBITDA might dip for a year. A stronger team and infrastructure can add far more value than the short-term hit costs you.

Green Flags and Red Flags Buyers Spot in the First Hour

We all do it. We pattern match quickly. Here is what lights up a buyer's dashboard fast.

Green flags

➡ The CEO brings a capable CFO or controller to the first meeting and lets them answer finance questions

➡ Clear org chart with defined accountability and real department leads

➡ Metrics that ladder from the front line to the board deck and tie cleanly to the P&L

➡ Evidence of professionalization over the last two years: key hires, systems implemented, board cadence

➡ Thoughtful story about where add-ons fit and a view of the pipeline

Red flags

➡ The owner insists on answering every question, including ones outside their lane

➡ Family members in most senior seats with no external bench

➡ Reports that require a translator to understand

➡ Customer concentration brushed aside as "they love us"

➡ Forecasts that move up when asked hard questions

None of this is personal. It is underwriting. Buyers are simply asking whether this business will perform after the check clears.

Choose Your Partner, Not Just Your Price

Price matters. It is usually the top factor for a seller. It should not be the only factor. If you plan to roll meaningful equity, you are picking a partner for the next hold period. Ask questions like:

➡ How often do you execute buy-and-builds in my sector?

➡ What resources will you bring on day one?

➡ What does year one look like in a typical 100-day and 12-month plan?

➡ Tell me about a deal that did not go to plan and how you handled it?

➡ Who will be on my board, and how do they operate?

When Everything Clicks

Every so often, you walk into a meeting and feel it in the first ten minutes. The company is professionally run. The numbers are clean. The team answers in their lanes. The systems are built for scale. The founder has built a machine that does not rely on heroics. Those companies have options. They can run a banked auction and let the market decide. They can run a quiet process and pick a partner. They can take a recap today and a second bite later. Options are leverage. Your job for the next few years is to build a company with options.

CHAPTER 6

QUALITY OF EARNINGS AND REVENUE

Now that we've introduced EBITDA and how it connects to valuation, it's time to dig into two of the biggest drivers of value in any private equity transaction: **quality of earnings** (QoE) and **quality of revenue**.

If you decide to sell your business and bring in an investment banker to represent you, one of the first things that will happen is an adjustment of your financials to reflect how investors think.

The banker's job will be to recast your numbers and calculate an EBITDA figure that tells the market, "Here's what this company is really earning." That number, along with the supporting narrative and other financial information, is then used to begin marketing the business.

Once a private equity firm becomes seriously interested, it'll issue a letter of intent (LOI) and then immediately hire its own independent adviser to do a **buy-side QoE review**.

This review typically involves the following:

- ➡ Non-recurring items – identifying and then adjusting for one-time events that can distort a company's performance.

- ➡ Revenue recognition/policies – assessing how and when revenue is recognized to ensure it's sustainable and that the numbers aren't being manipulated.

➡ Expenses – analyzing the company's spending patterns, including cost management and spending cuts that could contribute to long-term profitability.

➡ Cash flows – assessing the company's cash flows to confirm that earnings are supported by strong cash flows.

➡ Key Performance Indicators (KPIs) – Analyzing relevant operational metrics to understand performance drivers.

➡ Risks and Opportunities – Identifying potential challenges (such as customer concentration or capital expenditure needs) and opportunities (such as pricing opportunities or product/service expansion).

So, your financial information and analyses need to withstand scrutiny.

This diligence process is standard. Most mid-market buyers will spend tens of thousands of dollars (at their own expense) to validate your numbers. But here's the opportunity: smart sellers don't wait to be vetted. They get ahead of it.

That's why we strongly advise sellers to **conduct a sell-side quality of earnings review before going to market**. It's not expensive—usually in the range of $15,000 to $25,000 from a reputable firm—and it can help you catch issues before they become dealbreakers.

Unfortunately, this step is often skipped by founders or small investment banks who don't understand how rigorous the buyer's process will be. In our experience, 80%–90% of the deal books prepared by founders or local brokers contain significant errors—errors that erode buyer trust, create valuation gaps, and derail deals.

A sell-side QofE that stands to scrutiny matters because:

➡ It shows the market that you're prepared and professional.

➡ It sets realistic expectations and prevents you from anchoring to inflated numbers.

➡ It reduces surprises and protects you emotionally from post-LOI whiplash.

Quality of Revenue

Next, let's talk about the quality of revenue. This is the other major lever that can dramatically affect valuation—and even transactability.

At a high level, revenue quality is about **concentration, sustainability (that is, high customer retention), and reliability**.

One of the biggest red flags for investors is customer concentration. If your top two customers account for 40% of your revenue, or your top three make up 50% or more, that's a risk. The loss of even one customer could significantly impact your operations and business results.

So, what does best-in-class look like? In the eyes of an investor, an A-grade business is one where the top 10 customers account for less than 20% of total revenue—assuming those customers also:

➡ Pay on time

➡ Stay with you for many years

➡ Allow you to grow wallet share

➡ Accept annual price increases

That's high-quality revenue—sticky, diversified, and profitable.

Beyond concentration, buyers will also look at trends in individual customer profitability. Are you losing money on certain accounts? Are you serving clients who drag out payment terms and essentially use your business to prop up working capital? Those factors will show up in diligence—and they matter.

They'll also evaluate:

➡ Client tenure and renewal rates

➡ Upsell/cross-sell momentum

➡ Price elasticity and pricing power

➡ Overall margin consistency

All of this comes back to one key theme: **predictability of future cash flow**. The more predictable and sustainable your revenue, the more valuable your business becomes.

The Two Big Levers

Quality of earnings and quality of revenue are two of the most important levers you can control. Improve either one, and you're not just improving your valuation—you're also reducing risk, increasing buyer confidence, and making your business stronger.

A business with strong EBITDA but weak revenue quality might still sell—but not at a premium, and certainly not on your terms. A business with strong revenue quality but messy books might get offers—but offers will be discounted due to perceived uncertainty that increases risk.

If you want to be in the "wow" deal category—the kind of sale others will talk about-focus on these two levers.

Lessons from the Trenches of Platform Building

By Chris Santiago, CEO, Repairs Unlimited

I didn't take a straight path into private equity or platform operations. My early career began in regulation and took me through the stock market, professional services, real estate, and direct investment. At NASDAQ, I started on the listings side, working to bring large-cap companies to the exchange—through IPOs and competitive switches. It was there that I had my first real education in revenue diversification.

Our CEO at the time pushed us to think beyond transaction-based income. We started building a professional services division from the ground up—offering public companies tools they needed: press release distribution, earnings call support, investor intelligence, and governance platforms.

What started as an ancillary strategy turned into a real business. We scaled it to nearly $400 million in revenue. And, along the way, we realized these services weren't just for public companies—private ones needed them too. That journey taught me the fundamentals of creating value through acquisition, integration, and strategic adjacency.

The Makeover That Made Millions

When I left NASDAQ and stepped into the world of PE-backed platforms, I didn't ease in—I crash-landed straight into the operational deep end. No more slide decks or strategy sessions. This was boots-on-the-ground, sleeves-rolled-up leadership.

One of my first gigs? A legacy beauty brand we carved out from a public company. It had a name, some dusty IP, and a broken backend. We gutted it. Replaced the ERP. Rebuilt the supply chain. Rebranded the product line. Shifted everything to a 3PL. Within a few quarters, we'd grown the house brand's revenue 5x—and we didn't open a single new store. We just cleaned up the mess.

The s ecret s auce? P rofessionalization. I t w asn't fl ashy, bu t it wa s transformational. Most founders don't lose value because they aren't smart—it's because their systems are stuck in the past. They don't know their true unit economics. They don't have visibility by product, by channel, or even by region. And they're managing their business by gut feel instead of good data.

If you want to scale—or sell—buttoning up your operations isn't optional. It's the difference between running a nice lifestyle business and building a platform that someone will pay real money for.

The Turnaround and Exit When Founder and Family Dynamics Get in the Way

I worked with a family-run manufacturing business. It was a mess, literally and financially. Negative EBITDA. Negative cash in the bank. The business was being run into the ground, and the founder wasn't ready to let go, despite saying otherwise.

We got in, replaced the CEO, and built a cost Bible—line-by-line, what it cost to make each product. Turns out they were losing money on their largest customer (and on most customers) because they didn't understand their product costs. We restructured supplier contracts, raised prices, and within a year, the business was profitable and received a significant offer—10x projected EBITDA.

But...family dynamics torpedoed the deal—power struggles, second-guessing, unresolved succession. The CEO who turned it around quit. The deal died. And that company, as far as I know, may not survive. It's a stark reminder: succession planning isn't a theoretical exercise. You can't scale—or sell—without clarity on who's in charge and who's really ready to step back.

When Founders Stay On

One thing I see often is founders who've never had a boss. They built their business from scratch. Answered to no one. And then, suddenly, they're part of a PE-backed platform—with reporting obligations, Board meetings, and KPI dashboards.

It's a hard transition. Many struggle with it. Some fight it. A few adapt. If you want to stay on post-sale, be honest with yourself. Are you open to operating in a new environment? Are you coachable? Will you embrace structure, systems, and scale? If not, that's okay—sell and step out. But don't say you want to be part of the journey if you're not willing to change.

Scaling the Right Way

Today, I'm the CEO of a PE-backed restoration platform—fire, flood, and general contracting for insurance-related losses. It's a highly fragmented industry with real potential for roll-ups. The original founders ran the business by checkbook—no accrual accounting, limited systems, no CRM or ERP. We spent the first year building the foundation—cash flow forecasting, systems integration, org design.

Now we're actively acquiring. I speak with two to three founders a week. Many are sharp, gritty operators, but their businesses aren't sale-ready. Their accounting is built for tax minimization, not for clean EBITDA. They shift expenses across periods, run cash-basis books, and lack internal reporting.

In a Nut-Shell

If you're thinking about selling—or becoming a platform—my advice is this: get your house in order. Run your business like it's already owned by private equity. Then, when the call comes, you'll be ready.

The Big Ping

By Brendan Burke, Managing Director, Capstone Partners

Most sales of a business don't start with a bang, they start with a *ping*. You receive an email from an unknown fund with the subject line: "Potential Partnership." Or you get a voicemail from a corporate-development head: "We're interested in talking."

That's the doorway from operating to transacting. Suddenly, you're not just building the business, you're fielding a market. If that just happened to you, welcome to my world.

I've spent the last two decades at Capstone Partners helping founders and operators turn unsolicited interest into controlled, competitive processes. I joined in 2004 as a financial analyst when we were a tiny firm and did a little bit of everything. We've grown a lot since then, but my favorite seat is still the one I'm in now: talking to private equity all day, every day, and running sponsor coverage for a firm that sells more than a hundred founder- and family-owned companies each year.

This is the perspective I give owners when that first inquiry lands.

Start by Defining Success

Before you call anyone back, get clear on what "a good outcome" means for you.

Two questions I wish more owners led with:

1. **"What will this mean for my people and customers?"** If those are real priorities, say so up front. We'll screen buyers for operational fit, not just price, and we'll negotiate for the employment protections and transition support that matter to you.

2. **"What will my role be after close?"** Be honest with yourself. If you want to keep building with a partner, great—we'll target buyers who value that. If you want a clean break, say that now and design toward it. Misalignment here is what makes post-close miserable.

Build Value Long Before You Sell

I'm obviously biased toward the value of a good banker. Still true. But there's work you can and should do well before you hire me that will push valuation up and improve deal structure.

Three levers move the multiple most:

1. **Financial discipline.** If you can tolerate it, get an audit. At minimum, commission a third-party Quality of Earnings review before you launch a process. Clean statements, timely monthly closes, and a chart of accounts that isn't a mystery novel make buyers confident and lenders cooperative.

2. **Commercial system, not heroics.** If the founder is the sales engine, buyers see risk and cost. If there is a repeatable sales process—pipeline hygiene, quotas, conversion metrics, a forecast you consistently hit— buyers see scale.

3. **Less concentration.** One customer, one vendor, or one product line that drives half your revenue makes investors twitchy. Spread it out where you can. Each step away from concentration reduces perceived risk, which increases what someone can pay.

Those aren't cosmetic upgrades. They are the difference between "nice business" and "platform we can build on."

What I Actually Do

When people hear "sponsor coverage," it sounds abstract. Here's the practical version.

➡ **Market feedback.** While your deal is in market, we're on the phone with investors collecting reactions in real time—what's resonating, where the questions are, what proof they need. We loop that intel back to the deal team and adjust materials and strategy accordingly.

➡ **Sense-making.** Investor priorities evolve with cycles, regulation, lender appetite, and even the news cycle. We translate the noise: who is deploying, whose thesis fits your business, and who just changed direction last week.

➡ **Reach.** Warm calls beat cold teasers every time. Because we already speak to these firms daily, we can get your story in front of the right partners credibly and quickly.

That's our lane. Around it is the *village* that makes a transaction work.

It Takes a Village (And You Shouldn't Be the Project Manager)

A professional sale is not a real-estate closing with one agent. It's a coordinated effort run by your banker:

➡ **Core deal team.** Managing Director (your quarterback) supported by a Director, VP, Associate, and Analyst. The juniors do the heavy lift—spreading financials, normalizing owner add-backs, building the model, drafting the Confidential Information Memorandum, and standing up the data room.

➡ **Accounting partners.** Independent Quality of Earnings to "tick and tie" the numbers and reconcile all the one-time items that creep into family businesses.

➡ **Deal counsel.** Papering the LOI and the definitive agreement, negotiating reps, warranties, indemnities, escrows, and the thousand line items that convert headline price into *actual* proceeds.

➥ **Capital markets.** If the buyer needs debt, specialists corral banks and private credit lenders to finance the acquisition on competitive terms.

Your role in all of this is simple and hard: **hit your forecast.** The single best way to protect value is to keep running the company. Nothing reprices a deal faster than a miss mid-process.

How We Work with You When the First Knock Comes

Most founders call us after unsolicited outreach. That's smart. Even if you're "just exploring," assemble a small war room: experienced deal counsel, an accounting team for QoE, and a licensed investment bank. We'll turn one conversation into a controlled process with multiple options. That optionality is leverage, and leverage is value.

From there, we do the heavy lifting. We build materials that tell your story honestly and powerfully. We pre-screen buyers who actually fit your priorities. We manage diligence and timing so you don't get dragged into endless one-off requests. We protect your confidentiality and your time so you can keep selling, shipping, caring for patients—whatever you do best.

Choosing the Right Banker

There are a lot of us. Here's how I'd advise a friend to vet the team:

➥ **Make sure they're licensed.** Use a registered broker-dealer with FINRA-licensed professionals. Anything else is a red flag.

➥ **Look for depth, not a solo act.** A single impressive rainmaker without junior staff is risky. Deals need analytical horsepower and redundancy.

➡ **Insist on industry fluency.** The era of the generalist is over. Your banker should speak your market's language and have closed transactions in your vertical.

➡ **Check chemistry.** You're going to spend months together, including on days when someone has to deliver bad news. Pick people you trust and actually like.

If You're Even *Thinking* About It

If a transaction might be in your next 3–36 months, act like a company investors would love to buy:

➡ Close the books on time every month.

➡ Commission a QoE, and if you can, get an audit.

➡ Document the sales process and make it repeatable.

➡ Reduce customer and vendor concentration where possible.

➡ Build the bench that can run Monday after a Friday close.

➡ Decide your non-negotiables before a term sheet is in your inbox.

Do those things, and two outcomes improve: your valuation and your options.

Closing Thought

When that first email hits, you don't need all the answers. You need clarity on what a good outcome means for you, and a team that can translate your business into the language of institutional capital while you keep the numbers green.

CHAPTER 7

QUALITY OF LEADERSHIP

An owner-operator says, "I want a massive exit. I want to walk away with a pile of cash when the deal closes. And I want to retire."

That's a great goal. But when we ask whether they've groomed a successor, built out a leadership team, or stepped away from day-to-day operations, the answer is often not so clear.

If you're the founder and you want to exit fully, you're going to need to make yourself operationally irrelevant long before you leave.

The rule of thumb? It typically takes three years and three key people to replace the founder. That means building and empowering a leadership team that can function independently of you. Because when private equity buyers look at a business, they're not just evaluating the numbers—they're asking: *What happens if the founder leaves tomorrow?*

Let's be clear. Your business might have strong earnings. It might have recurring revenue. But if you're the one still making every major decision, calling every key customer and owning the relationship, and holding every leadership role in your head—you haven't built a business. You've built a job. And private equity doesn't buy jobs.

This is especially important for founders who want to retire and get all their cash at close. If there's no leadership team in place, it's going to affect the valuation. Sometimes by 20% to 30%. It will almost certainly affect deal structure. Instead of a clean exit with full cash at closing, you might end up with a third in cash, a third in an earnout over three years, and a third in rollover equity. The buyer is covering some of its risk by withholding cash in favor of performance-based compensation.

You may be grooming a successor, but that person will not take over until after the deal closes. If the successor is really prepared, why isn't he/she in place already? How will we know if this individual can deliver? How will the rest of the management team deal with the change? These are just a few sample questions, but we have seen too many deals fall through or be discounted because of poor succession planning.

Private equity investors don't just stop with CEO succession planning; they will look at the entire leadership team (potentially down to middle management). They will look at how roles are defined, how goals are set, how accountability is measured, and how employees are rewarded based on performance and merit. Loose accountability, loose measurement, less standardization and more tribal knowledge are not viewed favorably.

After the CEO (or President), the next critical position is the CFO. This individual needs to implement stronger financial controls to meet investor demands for fast monthly closes and accurate financial statements, along with relevant KPIs. In addition, since most PE transactions involve some debt financing, the CFO also needs to be ready to evaluate debt covenant compliance, including the ability to **forecast** it. Having the right CFO in place is critical to achieving a premium valuation.

Three Scenarios

Not every founder wants to retire. Most often, we see three leadership scenarios in PE deals:

1. **The Retiring Founder** – Wants to exit and retire, ideally with full cash at close. To get there, he needs a strong leadership team already

in place. Not a succession plan on paper—one that's in place and has been working for at least two years to deliver the results that are being marketed to potential investors.

2. **The Platform CEO** – This is the founder who isn't looking to walk away. Instead, she wants to partner with private equity to lead a buy-and-build strategy. She wants to be the platform company that acquires and integrates other businesses in the industry. These founders often stay on for multiple recapitalizations over a 10- to 15-year period. For them, private equity is fuel for scale—not an exit.

3. **The Roll-Up Partner** – These founders know they aren't the platform, but they see consolidation happening around them. They want to sell into a larger entity, roll equity, and stay on under new ownership. They may be a regional accounting firm joining a national roll-up, or a specialty HVAC company becoming part of a larger platform. These founders don't want out—they want in.

Each of these three archetypes—retiring founder, platform CEO, and roll-up partner—requires different preparation. And each one is viewed through a different lens by private equity.

If you want to retire and leave, the focus is on *replacement*—have you built a team that can run the business without you?

If you want to stay and scale, the focus is on *readiness*—do you have the leadership skills, systems, and vision to be a long-term partner in growth?

And if you want to join a larger platform, the focus is on *fit*—can you integrate smoothly into someone else's strategy?

No matter your intent, the leadership question is unavoidable. Private equity is investing in your team as much as your product. If your business can't thrive without you, it won't command a premium. But if you've built a team that can scale, lead, and perform independently, that's when the magic happens.

That's when you become the company everyone wants to buy.

How PE Reads Your Leadership

Private equity prices risk in the cash flow, and **leadership** is the first line of risk control. If you—the founder—still *are* the revenue engine and the operating system, the business is fragile. Fragile gets paid less cash and gets more structure (earnout, seller note, rollover). Proven leadership with a deep bench gets a higher multiple and more cash at close.

Here's how that gets judged in diligence:

1) Your timeline signals risk

If you want out in 6–12 months and you still own key customer relationships or daily operations, the buyer has to underwrite a management transition *after* close. That pushes value to contingency. If you're staying 3–5 years—or you've already installed a president/COO who's been running day-to-day for 12–24 months—risk drops, value rises.

2) The number of hats you wear is telling

In too many small companies, the CEO wears every hat: CRO, COO, CHRO. PE wants to see **clear owners** for revenue, operations, and people—each with measurable outcomes and the authority to act. If I can pull you out for a week and nothing material breaks, that's a green light.

3) Cadence beats charisma

Investors look for a management team that works well together and communicates across silos: weekly operations reviews, monthly financial reviews, and quarterly plan-forecast-retrospective analyses. That cadence is proof the team owns the results and is accountable—the only culture that scales.

4) Finance must be decision-grade

You don't need a fancy "strategic CFO" at sub-$5M EBITDA. However, you do need:

➡ **Accrual books closed on time** (lender-ready).

➡ **Unit economics** by job/customer so you can price, mix, and staff with intent.

➡ A **rolling forecast** with variance analysis and a record of how you changed behavior because of the data.

If financial statements are late, unreliable, on a cash basis, or opaque, everyone (including lenders) prices in uncertainty.

5) The room tells the truth

In diligence meetings, I watch who answers which questions. Best signal: the commercial lead talks pipeline quality, pricing, and net revenue retention; ops talks capacity and gross margin drivers; HR talks hiring velocity and regretted attrition; finance walks the close, unit economics, and the forward view. The CEO frames the strategy and lets them run with it. If the CEO answers everything, the team doesn't yet own it.

What to Do in the Next 12–24 Months

If you want options in a three-to-five-year window, run this play now:

1. **Install the right team.** Elevate or hire a real president/COO and let them own day-to-day outcomes. Give them the ball and the scoreboard.

2. **Move the top accounts.** Transition ownership of your ten largest customers to the team. Track retention and expansion to prove durability.

3. **Tighten controllership.** Hire the right CFO (if you don't have one). Close monthly on accrual by day 10; produce job/customer profitability; stand up a rolling 13-week cash view and a forward forecast.

4. **Lock the cadence.** Weekly ops, monthly financials, quarterly plan/forecast/retrospective analyses.

5. **Upgrade seats early.** If someone can't scale, make a change **before** the process begins. Self-aware replacements are a positive signal, not a red flag. If you can say, "Eighteen months ago we committed to a 3-year exit window. We upgraded these seats, changed our cadence, and here are the results," then PE hears *coachability*, not chaos.

"Give Them the Ball and the Scoreboard"

By Steve East, Chairman, CSM Group

For decades, I did what most founders do: build it myself, brick by brick. I bought the business when no one else would, leveraged my house, sweated through two shirts a day, and ran on instinct. We won work, did good work, and kept moving.

But there's a ceiling to founder-energy. If the future always has to pass through you, growth will eventually pass you by. So I set a new goal: build a company that could outgrow me.

By the time Seth called, we had the bones of a national business: deep relationships in food & beverage, healthcare, and pharmaceutical environments; a base in Kalamazoo that I believed could be a "center of excellence" supporting work across the country; and a leadership bench that was loyal, hardworking—and stretched. The next chapter wasn't about grit. It was about scale. I needed the right executive to turn a strong regional platform into a durable, nationally capable enterprise. Seth said he knew the person. He introduced me to Stuart Mason.

The Match that Mattered

Stuart came from running large divisions inside global organizations. If a recruiter had floated his résumé, I probably would've passed—too 'big-company' for us. But Seth vouched for the fit, and we met the next night. Stuart listened, asked sharp questions, and saw what Kalamazoo could be: not a constraint, but the back-of-house hub that powers national execution. He'd built that kind of hub before (his "Scotland center of excellence"). That was the picture I couldn't find in prior candidates.

We both took a bet. He on a founder-led company most people hadn't heard of. Me on a leader who hadn't grown up inside our culture. The bet paid. In just over four years, headcount grew from roughly a hundred to around 180, revenue accelerated significantly, and, more importantly, the caliber and cadence of the organization changed—weekly ops that drive outcomes, monthly financials we can manage to, a leadership team that makes decisions and owns them.

What I'd Do Again—and What I'd Do Differently

1) Pace the change.

We started fast—too fast. Day two we were interviewing lawyers; day three, we were moving pieces on a board we didn't fully understand. The intent was right: protect the company and go. The sequencing was wrong. If you're bringing in an outside leader, build a deliberate runway first to understand, then simplify, then act. Give them time to learn the people, the real capabilities, and the hidden constraints before you expect visible change. It will feel slow, but it's actually faster.

2) Set the score early.

Seth's advice in this book is dead-on: if you want options in three to five years, your first 12–24 months are about installing the right team, moving top accounts to the team, tightening controllership, and locking cadence. We did each of those—eventually. Doing them earlier would have reduced noise and increased trust. When a president arrives with a clear scoreboard and an agreed cadence, the organization rallies faster.

3) Upgrade seats before the process—not during.

Some people who were great for the first act won't scale in the second. That isn't a moral judgment; it's math. We raised the leadership bar and, in a few cases, raised our hands too late. Make the changes while you still have the calendar, not when a sale clock is running. Investors read proactive upgrades as coachability, not chaos.

4) Give the new leader real ownership.

A founder can't "half-delegate." About eighteen months in, I intentionally stepped back. That's when the flywheel clicked. Customers, employees, and partners need to see and feel who's running the company. As chairman, my job became clearing roadblocks, protecting culture, and holding the bar—not playing quarterback.

5) Tell the truth about the baseline.

If I could rewind, I'd hand Stuart a brutally honest brief before day one: here's what's excellent, here's what's fragile, here's what we don't know. He spent too much of the first season discovering things we could have simply stated. Candor compresses time.

What Changed inside the Business

Cadence replaced heroics.

We closed the books on time, reviewed profitability by job and customer, stood up a rolling cash view and forward forecast, and ran the business to plan instead of personality. Weekly operating reviews shifted from updates to decisions. That predictability is what buyers pay for—and what teams thrive on.

Enterprise accounts became team accounts.

I'd always been close to our largest customers. We made it a point to transition executive ownership to the team and to track retention and expansion. That proved durability beyond me and created headroom for growth.

Kalamazoo became a lever, not a label.

We embraced the "center of excellence" model: a strong hub with field execution where the work is. It's how you deliver national capability without losing cultural cohesion.

The leadership bench got deeper—and simpler.

Stuart is a positive, delegated leader. He sets expectations, supports the team, and insists on accountability. That combination let us raise standards without losing heart. We promoted where we could, hired where we had to, and organized around outcomes.

Lessons for Founders Staring at the Same Crossroads

- Hire for the next chapter, not the previous one. Don't look for a clone of yourself. Look for someone who has already lived where you want to go—and can translate that experience to your scale.

- Trust, then process. Your employees will take their cue from you. If you trust the new leader and show it, they will, too. Then install the operating rhythm that makes trust measurable.

- Sequence visible wins. Early, low-drama wins (clean close, on-time projects, a renewed master agreement) buy you runway for bigger changes.

- Protect the culture while raising the bar. Culture isn't a reason to avoid standards; it's the reason standards matter. The right leader will honor what's good and professionalize what's missing.

- Let go to grow. If every big decision still routes to you, you hired a lieutenant, not a president. Decide which you want. Your team will feel the difference.

Why this Matters for Value—Now and at Sale

Everything about shows up in valuation. Professional management, account durability, clean financials, and a repeatable operating system all reduce risk and increase the predictability of future cash flow. Whether you sell in two years or never, you've built a better business. And if you do sell, you've built one an investor can buy with confidence—at a better multiple and with cleaner terms.

Seth likes to say, "Give them the ball and the scoreboard." He made the introduction; Stuart took the ball; we installed the scoreboard. The result is a company that isn't dependent on a single founder, a team that wins on purpose, and a platform that can keep compounding—whether I'm in the room or not. That's the real enterprise value of a leadership transition done right.

The Operator Whisperer: Lessons from Both Sides of the Table

By Nicki Lambropoulos, CEO, Physician Directed Partners

When people ask me what it's like to lead a founder-run business through a private equity partnership, I usually say, **"It's a lot like a relationship."** There's the courting, the dating, the prenup, the marriage, the messy moments when you move in together—and then, if all goes well, you grow a family. I've lived every stage of that relationship, more than once, on both sides of the partnership. And I've learned exactly what makes it work—and what makes it fall apart.

I started my career as a CPA at a small firm in Chicago, where I spent years advising founder-led businesses. One of my longtime clients, a physical therapy practice, had grown organically to ninety locations over the ten years I worked with them. When they decided to sell to private equity, it was a first for everyone involved. No one, including the founders, fully understood what that would mean.

What felt like the very next day after getting "married," the "family" grew—fast. We went from 90 to over 450 locations almost overnight, thanks to their first and largest acquisition.

Less than three years later, we sold again—to a larger PE firm. I was now deeply embedded in the sell-side process. It gave me my first real taste of the other side of the table—and, honestly, it sparked an addiction. Being part of that process, understanding how and why we had operated and strategized the way we had over the previous years, was a lightbulb moment.

I joined them and began working directly with portfolio companies from LOI through exit. My focus has always been on **alignment, people, process, and technology**. And in that exact order. I believe there's an order to every successful "marriage" between founders and private equity:

➡ Alignment comes first. Without alignment—between the PE partner, the board, the management team, and the operators on the ground—you will never be able to get all parties aligned on strategy and where the business is headed. Lack of clear strategy and leadership mean you will have a challenge recruiting, growing, and retaining (essential) human capital.

➡ Without the right people, you won't build the right processes.

➡ Without the right processes, your data won't be reliable, no matter how advanced your technology is.

Every successful partnership starts with alignment. Everything else flows from there.

You Need the Right Partner—Not Just Someone Who Cuts a Check

Something I learned quickly, and keep preaching to founders today, is this: don't just chase the biggest check. Know who you're getting into business with. You wouldn't marry someone after one dinner—and a PE deal is a marriage. You need to meet the team, understand their decision-making style, talk to other founders they've worked with, and ask tough questions.

Founders often underestimate how much life will change post-deal. There will be a lender. There will be covenants. There will be new systems, new controls, new compliance expectations, new experienced team members, and a board that you will report to. And yes, there will be pressure.

The "Oh Shit" Moment

When do most people call me? It's usually after they've already gotten married—post-close—and they realize they weren't prepared. They didn't implement the right systems. They didn't hire the right people. Now the PE firm wants daily reporting, the lender needs clean audits, and the business can't even pull reliable metrics.

I call that the "oh shit" moment.

In an ideal world, you build for scale before the transaction. But in reality, many businesses skip that step. Maybe the capital partner assumed the founder had it covered. Maybe the founder assumed the PE firm would be more hands-on. That misalignment is where the wheels start to come off.

That's why alignment—true, documented, pre-close alignment—is non-negotiable. I tell founders all the time: put your three-to-five-year plan on paper. Agree on the growth strategy. Outline how you're going to get there. Talk about people, systems, incentives, everything. Treat it like a prenup. Because once you close, things will move fast—and the stakes will be higher.

Bridging the Emotional Gap

I've never been a founder. But I've spent enough time alongside them to deeply respect what's at stake. For most founders, the business is their baby. They've put in their time, money, energy, identity. When they sell—even if the check is life-changing—there's an emotional disruption that's real.

One common dynamic is a dip in performance during and after the deal. Sometimes it's burnout. Sometimes it's the psychological shift that comes from no longer being 100% in control. That's why structuring the right rollover equity and incentive plan matters—not just for economics, but to keep founders engaged and aligned. Incentives and alignment do not stop at founders—do not forget about your key employees, who are essential to getting you through stages.

There's also a culture shock. Suddenly, they have a Board. Maybe for the first time. And that Board has opinions. Timelines. Metrics. Opinions on their team. Sometimes the founder is no longer the right CEO—and if they're not prepared for that possibility, it can get rocky fast.

What I try to do is bridge the gap. Help the PE team understand what life looks like in the trenches. And help the founder understand what this new chapter really requires. Sometimes I feel like a therapist. Other times, a translator. But I'm always playing the middle, and I think that's why I've been able to help so many teams get through it without imploding.

Final Thought: Be Ready

If you're a founder thinking about a transaction, don't wait until PE knocks on your door. Get your house in order now. Build real systems. **Know your numbers—the key metrics that drive the business.** Pick 3-5 KPIs. Find a way to monitor them weekly, if not daily. Truly understand what drives value in your business, where the gaps are, and how to adjust.

And most importantly, find a partner who isn't just buying your business, but investing in your success. The right capital partner won't just hand you marching orders. They'll roll up their sleeves with you. They'll bring resources. They'll give you a sounding board. That's what partnership should mean.

Because once the deal is done, the real work begins—and you want someone in your corner when the "oh shit" moments come.

CHAPTER 8

QUALITY OF OPERATIONS

When private equity firms dive into diligence, they examine operations from a variety of perspectives. They're not just asking, *"How do you run the business today?"* They're asking, *"How well can this business scale without breaking?"* To answer that, they evaluate the **efficiency, scalability, and consistency** of your day-to-day execution.

In a company with strong operations, they expect to see documented, standardized processes, predictable results, sound cost control, and systems that allow the company to handle increased volume without sacrificing quality. Weak operations, on the other hand, show up in obvious ways: tribal knowledge, missed deadlines, poor customer satisfaction, high turnover, and bloated costs. Sloppy operations eat margin and destroy value.

What many owners don't realize is how thoroughly investors benchmark operational performance. If you're in an industry that PE has touched before (and most are), they already have benchmarks and know what the KPIs are. They know what an "A" looks like—and what a "C" looks like.

As an example, take a personal injury law firm. This firm may generate $1 million in annual revenue per lawyer. That sounds great until you ask:

➡ How many matters are you settling per year?

➡ What's the average file size?

➠ How many cases settle pre-litigation versus going to court?

➠ What's your customer acquisition cost and sign-up rate?

If you are in this space, you already know which KPIs drive profitability and margin, whether you measure them or not. Just know that private equity investors also know what the KPIs are in this industry and they will want answers during diligence.

In other industries, say commercial HVAC, the KPIs are different. Here, investors might study:

➠ How much time does a technician spend driving between jobs? What's your route density?

➠ Do your technicians have the parts and tools on hand to complete the job on the first visit?

➠ Is inventory managed well, with common replacement parts always on board? Are your trucks well stocked?

➠ For every dollar spent on preventive maintenance, how many additional repair dollars are found?

➠ How are you optimizing driving routes?

Investors also evaluate **third-party performance scores**. For example, in commercial HVAC, PE firms may analyze external performance metrics such as customer satisfaction, on-time arrival, work order completion rates, and safety records. In residential services, they may look at online reviews, Net Promoter Scores (NPS), or service-level compliance data from platforms like ServiceTitan. These objective measures help investors validate the company's internal claims and assess how well the business delivers consistent, measurable results to its customers.

Where Value Is Won or Lost

Private equity investors routinely assign **valuation discounts or premiums of 20% to 40%** based purely on operational strength. A messy, undisciplined business might still be profitable, but it will be heavily discounted. A tight, scalable business with professional systems and a strong culture? That's where the premium lives.

Consider labor. In a significant number of businesses, be it HVAC, plumbing, accounting, law, or janitorial, **labor is your most valuable—and volatile—resource**. If your operations are weak, your customers leave. And so do your people. In trades where technicians are already in short supply, high employee attrition is a killer. Replacing skilled workers is slow and expensive, and each departure eats into productivity, margin, and morale.

The inverse is also true: strong operations create stable teams. When customers are happy, they stick around. When teams are happy and well-utilized, they stay put. It makes a virtuous cycle: higher customer lifetime value, higher employee retention, and more reliable performance.

That's why investors care so much about who's running operations and how. Do you have a strong COO or operations lead? Are there documented procedures? Can the company maintain consistent delivery if a key person leaves or takes a vacation?

These questions all lead to the same point: **Operational excellence is how you win.**

Operational excellence determines:

- ➡ Whether you attract the right customers—and whether they pay well
- ➡ Whether your technicians or team members are efficient and effective
- ➡ Whether your business can scale without chaos
- ➡ Whether your EBITDA is worth an 8x multiple… or a 5x

Operational strength is also a direct reflection of leadership. It's not just *what* you do—it's *how well* you lead others to do it. Great leaders instill a strong culture, consistent performance, accountability, and a continuous-improvement mindset.

And all of this—the quality of your delivery, your customer base, your workforce stability—flows directly into your **financial reporting**, which is where we go next.

Because once an investor believes your operations are solid, the next question is: **Can you show me in the numbers?**

Operational Visibility and the Tech Stack That Supports It

Getting regular financial and operational reporting implemented into the business isn't hard—but it does require intentionality and investment. The good news is that in today's market, there are dozens of proven providers who know exactly how to do it for companies in the lower middle market.

There are industry-standard systems—reliable, affordable, cloud-based tools—tailored to companies just like yours. Whether you're in HVAC, legal services, home improvement, or any other trade or service business, chances are the technology already exists to help you track performance, spot bottlenecks, improve margins, and drive accountability. The tools are out there. The question is whether you've decided to use them.

And here's why it matters. If you're happy with how your business is running today, that's great. But when you begin thinking seriously about selling to a third party, you must understand that outside investors are looking at your business through a very different lens. Their questions are sharper. Their expectations are higher. And their tolerance for "we've always done it this way" without an explanation grounded in actual performance and metrics is close to zero.

That's why we encourage founders to address investments in the right technology now, before a buyer shows up. Weak reporting is easy to spot and easy to fix. We can point you to implementation partners across every industry who offer cost-effective pricing.

What you'll get in return is **visibility**: visibility into how your business actually runs. Where you're strong. Where you're leaking margin. Where your employees are thriving—and where they're not. The right tech stack isn't just about reporting. It's about operating and scaling efficiently.

For most companies, this means moving to a cloud-based system that supports core operational workflows, customer relationship management (CRM), and finance and accounting.

Even if you're not planning to sell anytime soon, these tools will make your company stronger. You'll run a better business. You'll spend less time chasing numbers and more time making decisions. And if or when the day comes that you do decide to engage with investors, you'll already be in a stronger position.

Why Outdated Systems (or No Systems) Kill Deals—and How to Fix Them

Old, unsupported systems—or worse, no systems—signal inefficiency and unnecessary risk. They suggest a company that's overly dependent on tribal knowledge or the founder's intuition. And for a buyer, they represent future disruption: the need to rip and replace, to retrain, to restructure workflows, to deal with downtime and data loss, and to address cultural pushback. That means costs. That means delays. That means a lower valuation.

Outdated systems also raise security concerns. Suppose your company is still running on-premise servers (literally data storage in your office or some old servers in the mechanical closet) with weak access controls. In that case, you're inviting cyber risk—and higher cyber insurance premiums under a PE owner. That's not an abstract concern. In diligence, these things come up. Buyers run scans. They ask questions. And if your tech stack is brittle, unsupported, or full of gaps, it's going to affect your transactability.

Here's what we want buyers to think when they see your systems: "We don't have to touch a thing." That means they can scale on top of what's already there. That means they can focus on growth rather than damage control. That means you get credit in the valuation.

To be clear: nobody's expecting perfection. You don't need to be running SAP like a Fortune 500 company. But you do need to have modern, stable, cloud-based systems. You need to be able to explain how your company tracks performance, assigns accountability, and makes decisions. You need to be able to show an investor what's happening in your business—without having to pull a rabbit out of a hat or run five separate Excel files.

Think of it this way: a good tech stack is like a well-built foundation. It's not flashy. It's not what your customers see. But it's what everything else is built on. And when it's solid, everything else gets easier: growth, retention, recruiting, compliance, profitability, and ultimately—value.

Playing For The Next Stage

By Gary Modrow, CFO, True Sports Group

I first met Seth when we were building E78 Partners into a purpose-driven growth company—focused on finance, accounting, and technology services for private equity funds and their portfolio companies.

What had begun as advisory work quickly expanded into fund administration, then full-scale back-office support. Our clients needed more, and we leaned in. The bigger vision was clear: to combine organic growth with a deliberate M&A strategy, scaling both capability and client impact.

Clarity Comes First

A lot of people approach growth and exits *reactively*. We didn't. From day one, we had a plan. Within 3–5 years, we wanted to hit aggressive growth targets—X to Y—and we knew getting there would likely require a private equity partner. Not someday. Soon.

We ran our first annual planning session under the EOS/Traction framework. That was the "aha" moment. Not because we had some magic epiphany, but because we finally had a shared language for what we were building toward. We all had ambition and horsepower, but this gave it structure. It gave us alignment. But that was not enough. We ended up developing a home-grown growth-to-partnership strategy that shares a lot of commonalities with Seth's Exit Value Realization System™. That's what propelled us to the next level.

That clarity paid off in every step that followed—internally and externally. Our team understood the goal. Our partners understood the timeline. And when we ultimately partnered with private equity, we weren't scrambling to clean things up or improvise strategy. We were ready.

Building the Right Pipeline

The E78 strategy was to find partners that were like-minded, who could deliver complementary services and create additional value for our clients. Client-focused growth for us meant cross-selling and bundling services to deepen our relationships with PE firms and their portfolio companies.

Together, we built out an M&A pipeline that gave us real options—not just deals to chase, but real fits to pursue.

What Makes a Good PE Partner?

In our space—back-office services for PE firms and their portfolio companies—the right partner needs domain expertise. That's non-negotiable. They have to understand the space, how it works, where value is created.

But even more important is alignment. Some PE firms are great at operational enhancement. Others are capital-structure artists. Some specialize in legacy business modernization—layering in technology and process. Whatever their playbook is, it needs to match the founder's vision.

You also have to know your role. Are you sticking around post-transaction? Taking a board seat? Rolling over equity and driving the next chapter? Whatever the case, you'd better be aligned with your new partner on expectations—and personalities. Professional fit matters. But personal compatibility matters just as much. A lot of the early process is *feel*. You sit across from someone and sense whether there's trust, honesty, and shared values. You can have all the diligence and structure in the world, but if the relationship doesn't work, the deal won't either.

What Breaks Deals

I've seen a lot of deals, both as participant and observer. Here's what kills them:

- ➡ **Misaligned expectations** – about valuation, roles, growth plans, timelines.

➡ **Culture clash** – even great businesses fail in PE if the cultural fit is off.

➡ **Ego** – whether it's overconfidence or insecurity, both can tank trust.

➡ **External disruption** – tariffs, trade policy, capital markets volatility.

Not every deal is meant to happen. And that's okay. One of the best outcomes is saying "no" early—professionally, respectfully, clearly. I've seen deals fall apart at the 11th hour... and then come back around months later, better timed, better aligned. But that only happens if you leave the door open with trust and transparency.

Why Preparedness Wins

The best transactions—without fail—are the ones where the founder and leadership team are truly prepared. Not just operationally. Emotionally.

If you've built a $20M, $50M, $200M company, you've poured yourself into it. You know your people. You've grown with them. So when it comes time to sell, you need to be clear on what you want. What you're walking away from. What you're walking toward.

And if there are multiple stakeholders—co-founders, family owners, investors—you all need to be aligned. That alignment, that shared conviction, will enable extraordinary success in the next chapter.

Great buyers can feel that preparedness. It builds trust. It lowers diligence friction. It accelerates decision-making. And it ensures no one's waking up with seller's remorse after close.

Tactical Readiness—and What Buyers Notice

At E78, one of our service lines was seller readiness consulting. But it's not just about cleaning up numbers. Tactical prep matters.

➡ **Clean financials**: Investors will pay more for a business that's organized and easy to understand.

➡ **Reliable reporting**: Confidence in past performance leads to confidence in future performance.

➡ **Scalable systems**: A buyer will value the readiness of your systems and the lack of investment they need to put into the business post-close.

➡ **Transparent communication**: The best founders tell their team early—"This is our plan." That transparency shows up in diligence and drives speed.

We've been on both sides of this. And I can tell you, buyers appreciate it. It lowers their costs, reduces risk, and often increases their willingness to pay.

Don't Wait

Many founders do not start a business with the intention of selling. But, if at some point you decide to pursue a transaction, you need to change your mindset and look at the business from a different perspective. You must look at it unemotionally, from the perspective of an investor or the next buyer. I know it is hard—as a founder I myself have had to make this shift. But if you can follow that guidance, the path becomes clear. Then it's just a choice about following it. Knowing exactly where you want to go next will inform everything, from who you hire and how you invest, to what you optimize and how you grow.

That's the only way you'll be ready—operationally, emotionally, and structurally—when the opportunity comes.

Today, I'm investing in and working with businesses that are in that same lower-middle market range. I want my experience in co-founding and exiting a business to help others in their journey. And I'm doing it with the urgency and discipline that comes from being in the fire—not just reading the playbook, but running the plays

Let's stop treating an exit like an afterthought. As soon as you realize that's what you want, it's the driving force of the strategy. And the sooner you own that, the better the outcome will be.

The Hard Truths of Selling

By Gary Baughman, Partner, Samson Partners Group

I've spent the last nine years of my career deep in the private equity world. Sometimes I'm the CEO of a PE-backed company. Other times, I'm sitting on a board, advising sponsors on acquisitions, or serving as an operating partner helping portfolio companies get their house in order. Most of my work has been in the lower middle market—companies with less than $10 million of EBITDA. For many of the founders I work with, their first encounter with private equity is exactly that: their first. The maiden voyage.

And I can tell you, it is not a smooth cruise.

Too many sellers walk into this process unprepared, starry-eyed about valuation, and blind to the realities of life after the deal. My goal here is not to scare you, but to give you a brutally honest look at what's ahead, so you don't step into the same traps I've seen over and over.

Start Before the Banker

If you take nothing else away, take this: the time to get serious about selling is years before you hire a banker.

Before you sign an LOI, before you even make the decision to sell, you need to sit with yourself and ask some agonizingly tough questions.

➥ Why am I selling?

➥ Have I truly explored all my options—succession within my family, a management buyout, even just slowing down and building a stronger team?

➥ What will I do after I sell? Will I stay in the business? For how long? In what role? Under what conditions?

→ What happens if the deal doesn't go as planned—if the company underperforms, or if I wake up six months in and realize I hate working under a PE sponsor?

Most founders skip these questions. They charge ahead, driven by pride in what they've built and dollar signs in their eyes. But private equity is not just a transaction. It's a marriage, and like any marriage, you'd better know who you're marrying and what life is going to look like afterward.

Seek wise counsel. Not just from a banker trying to win your mandate, but from people who have walked this road before. Ask other founders what they wish they had known. Ask trusted advisors to play devil's advocate. And be honest with yourself about what kind of environment you thrive in, because after the deal, you will not be in charge anymore.

The Banker "Problem"

Let's talk about sell-side bankers.

What bankers should be doing is educating you from day one. They should explain:

→ The time and effort you personally will need to invest.

→ The cost of the process.

→ The gaps in your reporting, systems, and management team that buyers will seize on.

→ The reality of valuation multiples, and what drives them.

Nine times out of ten, that education never happens. Instead, sellers go to market woefully unprepared. Their data is sloppy. Their systems can't produce the level of reporting buyers demand. Their management bench is thin. Their growth strategy is more wishful thinking than tactical plan. All of this translates directly into a lower multiple, because buyers perceive risk—and they price risk.

And then there's the Confidential Information Memorandum (CIM). Don't get me started on the CIM. This is supposed to be the story that shines a light on the true business you're trying to sell, portraying it in a concise and genuine manner. Instead, ninety-five percent of them are garbage: inflated EBITDA, fantasy forecasts, hyperbole about "tailwinds" and "resilient markets," and no honest discussion of risks or challenges. Everyone in the industry knows it, yet the charade continues.

Here's the problem: when buyers read a CIM that's clearly puffed up, you create distrust right out of the gate. And once distrust enters the relationship, it never leaves. Buyers hedge against that distrust with lower offers. If you want to maximize your valuation, you need transparency, not spin.

What Diligence Really Feels Like

If you think diligence is just a paperwork exercise, you're in for a rude awakening.

The diligence process is cloak-and-dagger, unnecessarily drawn out, and exhausting. It will consume at least half of your day, every day, for months. If you don't delegate more of your operating responsibilities ahead of time, your business will suffer at exactly the moment you need it to look strongest.

Buyers will demand access to your next level of management. Founders often resist this, worried about spooking their teams. But hiding your people only adds risk to the deal. Buyers want to see the competence of the bench. If they can't, they assume the worst—and discount their offers accordingly.

Buyers will also focus on the outliers: your largest contracts, newest products, riskiest initiatives. They will poke at those, particularly if they're convinced you either misrepresented them or underestimated the risk. If your answers are defensive or dismissive, you poison the relationship. I've seen it happen. One founder, confronted with tough questions about massive new contracts, bristled at the scrutiny. The buyer backed off rather than blow up the deal. Months after close, those contracts imploded, and litigation followed. Everyone lost.

The point is not that you should avoid risk. Business is risk. The point is that you must present those risks honestly, with context, and with humility.

The Succession Mirage

Another gaping hole in most deals is succession planning.

Founders tell buyers they'll stick around for two years to transition the business. Then, six months later—burned out from the new demands of PE ownership and flush with liquidity—they head for the exit. I don't blame them. Life under PE is heavier: constant reporting, board meetings, debt covenants, strategy sessions, system upgrades, weekly calls. It's a different world.

But when founders bail early, it throws the company into chaos. The informal successor they promised to groom is left stranded. The PE firm, unwilling to gamble on unproven talent, hires from the outside. The culture jolts, momentum stalls, and value erodes.

The only way to avoid this is through brutal honesty and scenario planning up front. If you think there's any chance you won't last two years, say so. If you're open to staying but only in a defined role, spell that out. Document what happens to your equity or earnout if you leave early. Don't assume "gentlemen's agreements" will carry the day—they won't.

Do Your Own Diligence

Founders love to talk about the diligence buyers put them through. But what about your diligence on the buyer?

Too few sellers take this seriously. They rely on their banker's assurances or the warm glow of a steak-dinner meeting. That's not diligence.

You should be calling CEOs who have run companies for that PE firm. Ask them what life was really like. Did the sponsor deliver on its promises? Were they fair partners? Did they invest in growth, or just cut costs? Call bankers who have closed deals with them. Call other founders who've exited to them.

You should also scrutinize your sell-side advisor with the same rigor. What deals have they closed? How did those companies fare two years later? Talk to their past clients. If you don't, you're abdicating one of the most important decisions of your life.

And finally—look in the mirror. Strip away the pride and the dollar signs. Are you truly ready to sell? Not just financially, but emotionally? Because once the ink is dry, there is no going back.

The Coat of Humility

This may be the hardest lesson of all.

Founders are proud of what they've built. Rightly so. But that pride often curdles into defensiveness the moment buyers start asking probing questions. They bristle when outsiders suggest better systems, more professional management, or a clearer growth strategy. They hear it as an attack on their competence.

It's not. It's simply reality. There are things you don't know. There are ways your business could be stronger. That's not a judgment—it's an opportunity.

If you can put on what I call a "coat of humility," you'll navigate this process with far less stress. Instead of seeing diligence as an inquisition, see it as a chance to learn how others view your business and how it can grow. Instead of treating every question as an insult, treat it as data.

I've watched too many founders turn what should be the most exciting moment of their professional lives into an anxiety-ridden ordeal—simply because they couldn't stomach the idea that someone else might improve their baby. Don't make that mistake.

It's Up to You

All of the pitfalls I've described—unrealistic CIMs, unprepared sellers, neglected succession, poor diligence, defensive posturing—can be mitigated if founders get the right counsel early. The kind of counsel that doesn't just chase a transaction fee, but that walks you through the realities and helps you prepare.

It's not free. It takes time, humility, and hard work. But the payoff is enormous: a higher multiple, a smoother process, and peace of mind when the dust settles.

And if you want my final piece of advice: don't wait until the banker comes calling. Start now. Because whether you sell in one year or five, the work you do today will determine whether that sale is the proudest moment of your career—or the most painful.

CHAPTER 9

QUALITY OF FINANCE AND ACCOUNTING

When it comes to how investors assess your business, few areas matter more than finance and accounting. This is the lens through which every operational strength—or weakness—is identified and/or validated. It's the substance that supports the story. No matter how compelling your leadership, loyal your customers, or promising your growth, if the financials are unclear, incomplete, or unreliable, buyers will hesitate.

Investors don't just want to know that your business is profitable—they want to know *how* it makes money, how predictably, and with what margin of safety. Financial clarity builds confidence. Without it, deals slow down, terms get tougher, and valuations take a hit.

So, what do we mean by "quality of finance and accounting"?

It starts with financial transparency. In founder-led businesses, especially in the lower middle market, it's common to see companies that manage the business off bank statements and only pull together financials once a year at tax time. That may work for an owner-operator running lean and cash-based. But an outside investor needs more.

Buyers want to see accurate, timely, and repeatable reporting. That means closing the books monthly in a reasonable time frame (generally in 7-10 days). It means generating internal financial statements at least quarterly. It means not just tracking the P&L, but also understanding the balance sheet, cash flows, working capital needs, and relevant KPIs that drive accountability. A business with robust financial reporting is typically one where the owner understands what's driving profitability—by service line, by customer, and by employee.

Strong financial reporting also helps you manage seasonality. In industries with cyclical revenue patterns—like HVAC, landscaping, or even personal injury law—PE buyers want to understand how you manage the off-season. Are you carrying excess labor? Are you adjusting expenses accordingly? Can you manage overhead and still deliver acceptable margins even in your slowest quarter? These are all questions good financial data should be able to answer.

If your reporting is poor or nonexistent, it can significantly reduce your valuation. If it's decent but not investor-grade, you'll likely end up somewhere in the middle of the range. But if your reporting is excellent—if you can provide reliable monthly financials, solid forecasting, strong KPIs, and consistent EBITDA normalization—you'll stand out. That kind of transparency and discipline puts you in the "A" bucket and helps command a premium.

It's also important to separate financial reporting from cash management. Accounting is one thing; understanding and forecasting cash is another. Most founder-led businesses in say, sub-$50M in revenue—are debt-free and run their companies based on cash in the bank. That works, until you try to sell to private equity.

Why? Because PE buyers almost always use leverage. They finance acquisitions with a mix of equity and debt. And that debt has to be serviced—from the cash flow of your business. If buyers can't get a clear picture of your cash cycle, they may hesitate—or worse, they may need to structure a deal that includes an earnout, seller financing, or other risk-sharing terms to mitigate that uncertainty.

Working capital management and cash clarity matter. Investors want to know:

- Are bonuses accrued properly and paid on a predictable schedule?

- How are overtime and hourly labor costs managed?

- If your business uses inventory, how is it tracked and replenished?

- If you have a fleet, are vehicles owned or leased? Maintained in-house or by third parties?

- Are A/R and A/P aging, cash collections and disbursements appropriately managed?

Weak cash management signals risk. If investors can't trust that the business can carry a reasonable debt load—or if they suspect they'll need to inject working capital after closing—it can directly impact both valuation and structure. At best, they'll price it into the deal. At worst, they'll walk.

Pricing cash flow uncertainty into the deal may mean less cash up front and tying a larger share of the total value to performance-based payouts. That's not necessarily a bad thing—many sellers agree to earnouts or seller notes—but poor financial visibility makes those mechanisms feel like protection, not partnership.

The good news? Your finance and accounting infrastructure can be upgraded long before you go to market.

Best-in-class finance and accounting for a lower middle market business has:

- **Monthly closings and clean books.** Not perfect GAAP compliance, but real structure and consistency.

- **Clear normalization of EBITDA.** Adjustments that are well documented and supported.

- **Cash flow forecasting.** Especially important if there's seasonality or working capital swings.

- **Linkage between operational metrics and financial performance.** If you have reporting that shows productivity, it should tie to revenue and gross margin.

➡ **Scenario modeling.** A basic ability to run "what if" analyses and show resilience under various growth or risk assumptions.

The bottom line? If your books are a mess, or your cash position is always a surprise, you're not ready for PE. But if your financial house is in order—and your reporting tells the story of a healthy, disciplined company—you're already ahead of the pack.

Getting Real about a Real Business

By Bryan Bloom, CPA, Owner/CEO, Howard, Nunn, & Bloom

I've sat on both sides of the table. I've worked on M&A deals as a consultant. I've helped clients prep for exits. I've been behind the curtain, seen the math, the deal docs, the "congrats" emails. But it's different when the target is you.

Today, I own a boutique CPA and advisory firm, and I'm quietly exploring what a partnership or capital event might look like. So I understand exactly what this book's audience is feeling—because I'm living it too.

And I can tell you this: the biggest mistake most owners make is thinking they have more time. They say they want to exit in three to five years, but they act like the clock hasn't started ticking. The truth is, the three-year runway starts now. And if you wait until you're in the process to get serious, you're going to leave a lot of value on the table.

That's not theory. That's what I've seen over and over again.

The Price of Being Unprepared

When I was doing M&A advisory, I saw this same movie play out all the time: a business owner gets a bite from private equity and thinks, "Okay, it's go time." They talk valuation, start imagining the number they're going to walk away with—and start mentally spending it.

But then the diligence phase begins. And it gets ugly fast.

Suddenly, the buyer's team is digging into things the seller hasn't looked at in years: lease structures, client concentration, compliance gaps, state tax exposure, embedded liabilities. You thought your EBITDA was $3 million? Turns out it's $1.8 million once it's been scrubbed.

I've watched this derail deals—or worse, push founders into accepting terms they never would've accepted at the beginning. Because emotionally, they were already out. They told their spouse. They shopped for the lake house. They let the fantasy run wild. And when reality didn't match, they just… compromised.

That's the risk of not getting your house in order early.

The Key Questions Owners Avoid

There are a few big questions I think every owner—especially in a professional services firm like mine—needs to ask long before they even think about transacting.

First: What happens if you disappear tomorrow?

That's succession in its rawest form. Are you the rainmaker, the client relationship manager, the technical expert, and the person approving payroll? If so, you're not an owner. You're a bottleneck. No one's buying that risk.

I've had to look in the mirror on this myself. In my firm, we do a lot of fractional CFO work. I've got clients where I have full access to their bank accounts, their systems, their offices. That's not a relationship you can hand off to a junior associate with a handshake. There's trust. There's continuity. And if I don't solve for that—by building a team, delegating delivery, and institutionalizing the client relationships—then the firm isn't worth much beyond me.

Second: What's really in your book of business?

A lot of CPA firm owners think their client roster is rock solid. But a real buyer's going to peel it back and ask: How concentrated is your revenue? Are these recurring relationships or one-off tax clients? Are the businesses you serve growing or aging out? Are you full of retirees? Are you one client loss away from a 20% haircut?

If you haven't already pressure-tested that book—and taken a hard look at profitability, retention risk, and long-term stickiness—you're flying blind.

Third: Are you willing to be honest about culture and fit?

One of the biggest traps I've seen in small business deals is ignoring the cultural red flags. In the first few meetings, everyone smiles. Everyone's agreeable. But that doesn't mean you're aligned.

I've seen deals fall apart because the seller didn't do the work to understand how the other side really operated. Or worse—they closed and then found themselves in a miserable working relationship, stuck with a post-close earnout and misaligned expectations. Once you're married, it's hard to walk away.

You've got to spend time with the people. You've got to talk through how decisions will be made, how autonomy works post-close, and what happens when there's friction. Because there will be friction.

In This Market, PE Wants a Real Business

Let's start with the problem nobody in public accounting likes to admit: the best rainmakers are often the worst succession planners. If 30% of your revenue comes from clients who will only dial your cell phone, you're not building equity—you're stockpiling liability. A PE buyer doesn't want to inherit your calendar; they want to inherit your cash flow.

Let's be clear: private equity doesn't want to buy a job. They want to buy a business. A system. A machine.

That means:

➡ Clean financials

➡ Documented processes

➡ Delegated authority

➡ Strong second-tier leadership

➡ Reliable, predictable cash flows

And increasingly, they want leverageable platforms. In the CPA and advisory world, that might mean a firm that's ready to grow regionally, add on other firms, and scale beyond the founder. I've talked to buyers who are actively looking for that—firms they can turn into a platform, not just bolt onto one.

For someone in their 40s or 50s like me, that's exciting. That's a chance to double-dip: sell once, then help scale it and sell again. But only if you're willing to play the long game and build the right infrastructure now.

Deal Structures Are Built on Assumptions

Here's another thing people miss: the deal you're promised on Day 1 is not the deal you close.

Private equity loves to talk big upfront—7x EBITDA, big earnouts, second bites of the apple. But read the fine print. That earnout might require 35% year-over-year growth for three years straight. That 7x valuation might assume an adjusted EBITDA you can't actually sustain.

I recently talked to a buyer offering exactly that. Big number. Great headline. But when I broke down the math, the milestones were ridiculous. If I didn't hit those hockey-stick projections, I'd leave millions on the table.

That's not a partnership. That's a setup.

So you've got to be realistic. You've got to push back. And you've got to know your numbers cold—because if you don't, they will. And they'll use it.

Where the Right Partner Changes the Game

When I think about what makes a deal actually work, it comes down to one thing: the right partner.

A good capital partner brings more than money. They bring focus. They bring resources. They accelerate your plans instead of replacing them. But only if you're aligned—strategically, culturally, and emotionally.

That's why I've reconnected with people like Seth recently. We'd known each other loosely for years—his wife was actually my first boss at PwC. But when I bought this firm and started thinking about growth, I reached out to him because I know he and the team at Samson had tremendous experience in my space, and I know him as a person and as a fellow founder - with deep empathy and understanding, he asked questions. He challenged my assumptions. And he's helped me think through not just how to grow, but why.

We've spent time discussing what I want my company to be, what I want to create, and how to architect the firm so that it is ready for Private Equity investment should I go down that path. I also know I will be an add-on to an existing business, not a platform. I am clear on that and what it entails. I am taking the realistic view of myself and my firm relative to the market, and this is enabling me to be very deliberate about how we grow and operate and position ourselves for the next phase of our journey, as part of an investor-backed platform. The system that Seth and the team at Samson have created feels like it was tailored for me: it really has created the grounding force from which I am operating.

There are a lot of shiny objects in this space. A lot of buyers, a lot of money, a lot of pressure to transact fast. But if you don't know what you really want—and if you don't have someone in your corner who will call BS when it matters—you're going to lose your footing fast.

I've seen it too many times.

And that's why, when you're playing the long game, you start today.

From "We'll Figure It Out" to Sale-Ready

By Jordan McMillian, Partner, Samson Partners Group

"We need to professionalize."

If you run a $10 – $75 million services business, you've probably said that sentence—or muttered it under your breath—more than once. You can feel the ceiling, but you can't quite see it. Revenue grows, headcount grows, complexity explodes, and suddenly you're spending your weekends fixing what broke on Tuesday. That's usually when my phone rings.

Fifteen years ago Seth hired me into a 97-country engineering giant. We bonded over process, operations, and the odd fact that I broke up with my boyfriend on the way to the interview because I knew the job would put me on planes every week. Since then, I've installed the same foundational playbook at IBM, Degree One, E78 Partners, and—most recently—as acting COO for four owner-operated companies preparing to sell or recapitalize.

Here's what those founders had in common:

➡ An asset worth eight figures—tied to a leadership structure worth five.

➡ A conviction that "operations" is a back-office chore, not a value lever.

➡ A dream of exiting in six months—when the real runway is closer to twentyfour.

Why Writing It Down Changes Everything

I start every engagement with the least sexy question in business: *What do you have written down?* Roles, responsibilities, checklists, KPIs, handoff triggers, client-ready deliverables—show me the receipts. Eight times out of ten, there aren't any. Not because the team is lazy, but because tribal knowledge feels faster—right up to the moment you try to scale.

Once we drag the work out of everyone's head and onto paper (or whiteboard, or Miro board) the founder sees the hidden friction: duplicate approvals, undocumented billable time, revenue leaking rework, heroic employees masking broken processes. And that's when the discomfort hits.

Document every repeating task, every recurring decision, and every client facing deliverable. Count how many depend on you personally.

Most owners want the *outcome* of documentation—lower error rates, faster onboarding—without the grind of documenting. There's no shortcut.

Tearing the Process Apart (Without Harming Each Other)

Documentation alone doesn't move the valuation needle. We have to break the workflows and rebuild them for speed, margin, and repeatability. That means weeks of "Why?" questions:

- Why does invoicing start on Day 6 instead of Day 1?
- Why does Sales own scoping when Delivery owns the margin?
- Why does every custom project default to reinventthewheel mode?

Founders hate this part. It feels like judgment. In truth it's liberation: every inefficiency we kill today is one less discount the buyer will demand tomorrow. The friction can last two quarters. But, in the third quarter, the organization stabilizes and the early wins show up in the numbers—lower DSO, higher gross margin, fewer all-hands emergencies.

Staff It Right or Stay Forever

By the end of Year 1, the playbook exists, the kinks are ironed out, and one fact becomes impossible to ignore: **If you are still the lynchpin, you're also the discount.**

Institutional buyers pay for durable cash flows, not heroic founders. If you plan to roll 2040 percent of your equity and keep running the company, terrific—the buyer will love your energy. But if you dream of handing over the keys at closing, we need a leadership team that can carry the weight without you. That means:

1. A president or CEO who has logged at least one full fiscal year in the seat—budget, P&L, and board pressure included.

2. A real CFO (or VP Finance) who can close books within ten days, answer lender questions in real time, and defend every penny of EBITDA.

3. A revenue leader who can explain **how** an extra $5 million turns into booked business—channel by channel, SKU by SKU—without you in the room.

Get that trio humming and your "keyperson risk" story evaporates. Skip it, and you'll finance your own exit via an earnout.

Earnouts: A Potential Poison Pill You Can Avoid

Earnouts exist to bridge valuation gaps. They rarely feel like a *bonus* to the seller; they feel like a leash. Miss a covenant because a key customer delays payment? That escrowed payout vanishes. Hit 95 percent of target instead of 100? Good luck renegotiating.

The surest antidote is proving the business will thrive without you. When a buyer believes the team, systems, margin, and pipeline are already derisked, cash at close rises, and contingent comps shrink. I've seen founders add two full turns of EBITDA to the upfront price simply because they invested in a real COO and CFO a year before going to market.

When Founders Stay On

Not every owner wants to ride off into the sunset. Some want a "second bite." If that's you, everything we've already covered still matters—because you're about to have a boss for the first time. Board decks, KPIs, budget reforecasts, integration meetings: they all arrive on Day 1 post-close. The disciplined operating cadence we install presale is exactly what keeps you sane—and keeps the buyer from parachuting in their own operators.

A Cautionary Tale and a Success Story

Case 1—The Sprint That Tripped.

A $32 million consultancy tried to sell six months after signing their LOI with a banker. Month end closed on Day 35, pipeline data lived in spreadsheets, and the founder still approved every proposal. The buyer uncovered $1.2 million in write-offs, dropped the price by 25 percent, and insisted the founder stay three years with a tiered earnout. He accepted—then called me six months later asking how to dig out.

Case 2—The Slow Burn Win.

A $48 million specialty contractor took the full two-year runway. We hired a CFO, implemented NetSuite, cut DSO by twelve days, and promoted a president who drove margin from 14 % to 18 %. When they finally ran a process, we fielded nine IOIs, four LOIs, and closed in 97 days—95 percent cash at close, 5 percent rollover, zero earnout. The founder stayed on as chairman, works two days a month, and spends the rest of his time fishing.

The Payoff

Professionalizing feels mundane in the moment—spreadsheets, SOPs, huddles—but the payoff compounds. Faster closes mean cleaner diligence. Defined roles mean sustainable growth. And when the term sheet lands, you negotiate from strength, not hope.

So wherever you are in the cycle, remember: write it down, tear it apart, staff it right. Do the unsexy work now, and the shiny deal later will shine a lot brighter—whether you stay for the second bite or sail into the sunset.

And if you're still tempted to sprint? Call me after your third all-nighter chasing data you thought existed. I'll be the one reminding you that professionalism is just discipline—applied long before the banker shows up.

CHAPTER 10

QUALITY OF GROWTH

Not all growth is created equal.

This is one of the most fundamental truths in private equity—and one of the most misunderstood. A business might be growing, but the *quality* of that growth is what ultimately determines its valuation, deal structure, and investor appeal.

Let's say your industry is growing at 5% annually. If your business is only growing at 3%, you're underperforming to the market. That signals: potential issues in your operations, market approach, customer mix, or pricing power.

Strong growth, meanwhile, whether organic or inorganic, signals operational excellence, market relevance, and leadership capability. Let's start with organic growth—growth that comes from your business today by winning new customers, expanding wallet share of existing customers, and increasing prices over time.

Organic Growth: Outpacing the Market

If your market is growing 4%, and you're growing 8–12%, you're probably taking share. If you're also delivering 3–5 percentage points more in EBITDA margin than the average competitor, you're likely running a best-in-class business.

What High-Quality Growth Looks Like

From an investor's lens, quality growth isn't just about top-line expansion. It's about *how* you grow:

→ **Diversified Customer Base**: Are you winning new clients while also expanding wallet share with existing ones? A business that's doing both is delivering value and being recognized by the market.

→ **Customer Concentration Risk**: Ideally, your top 10 clients shouldn't make up more than 20% of total revenue. Too much concentration increases downside risk.

→ **Pricing Power**: Can you increase prices annually—at least in line with inflation—without losing customers? Better yet, can you price above inflation and justify it through quality and service? That's real pricing power.

→ **Stickiness & Retention**: How long do customers stay? How often do they renew? Do they increase spend over time? Investors look closely at retention and upsell metrics to assess revenue durability.

→ **Margin Integrity**: Growth that sacrifices EBITDA is not high-quality growth. Discounting to win customers or running a loss-leader model that doesn't eventually drive profitability will hurt your valuation, even if revenue is growing.

Growth vs. Profitability Tradeoffs

A common trap is celebrating growth without tracking margin compression. For example, some businesses pursue aggressive growth by underpricing to win customers, planning to make it up with add-ons later. That can work *if* the pull-through revenue materializes and *if* the strategy is evident in the financials. But if top-line growth is outpacing EBITDA, and there's no clear plan to reverse that, it raises a red flag.

Likewise, if you're growing revenue but at a rate below the market's growth rate, your relative position is slipping. You're losing share—and that's a warning sign.

Why It Matters to Investors

Private equity firms aren't just buying where you are—they're betting on where you can go. And growth is the engine of future returns. But they want that engine to be:

➡ Efficient (margin-accretive)

➡ Predictable (low churn, strong renewals)

➡ Defensible (customer loyalty, pricing power)

➡ Scalable (systems and people to support more volume)

Quality growth, in this context, is about building a business that's not only expanding, but expanding in the right way.

In short, investors don't just want to see your revenue chart go up and to the right. They want to know how steep the slope is, what's powering it, and whether it's sustainable. High-quality growth tells a compelling story—and earns a premium multiple.

Inorganic Growth: Acquisition Experience as a Value Lever

The next critical dimension of growth we often assess is **inorganic growth**—that is, growth through acquisition. For many founders, this is an evolution they usually explore, especially once organic channels start to plateau or when opportunities arise to consolidate local or regional competitors.

Some founders choose to pursue acquisitions on their own—before involving any private equity backing. When executed well, these deals can be transformational. The businesses that successfully integrate targets, retain key customers and employees, and build a cohesive culture post-acquisition often see significant boosts in both scale and valuation.

From an investor's perspective, this experience can be a real asset. If you're seeking to position your company as a platform for future roll-ups, demonstrating a strong M&A track record *matters*. Likewise, if you've built relationships with other potential sellers and have a viable acquisition pipeline, that can be highly attractive to PE firms—especially those seeking to deploy capital quickly in a fragmented market.

This kind of experience may also affect your deal structure too. A strong M&A history can justify a higher valuation or deliver value through an earnout, seller equity rollover, or a performance-based bonus tied to future acquisitions.

That said, a *bad* acquisition experience is often worse than no acquisition experience at all. If you've tried a deal that failed—resulting in culture clashes, customer loss, or poor financial outcomes—it can impair your transactability. Investors will likely worry about what they need to unwind or fix. If you've gone through this, it's essential to demonstrate that lessons were learned and the business has stabilized since.

So while inorganic growth isn't a requirement for a successful transaction, it can be a powerful value lever—*if executed well* and *proven over time.*

What I Learned Selling To PE, Getting Fired, and Buying Businesses

By Matt Matros, Serial Entrepreneur

I started a smoothie bar in Chicago, turned it into a fast-growing chain called Protein Bar, proved it could work in a second market in Washington, D.C., and then sold a majority stake in 2013 to L Catterton, a top consumer private equity firm. That closing day not only turned me into a millionaire, it's also the day I took on a formal role, *becoming the CEO of a PE-backed company*. A year later, I was out of the job at the company I founded.

The Setup

By 2012, we were a twenty million dollar run-rate business, portable across markets, and sitting at the intersection of two investor obsessions at the time: health and wellness, and fast casual. In PE courtship terms, we were the hot girl at the dance. Inbound calls came from the usual suspects. I built relationships, compared offers, and picked Catterton because I liked the partner, I respected their track record, and they also put up the best numbers for me and the company.

I owned roughly half the business pre-deal. They bought 60 percent. I rolled a large chunk of my equity and stayed on as CEO. From the first serious conversations to close was about eighteen months. For consumer acquisitions, that cadence felt normal.

On September 30, I was an entrepreneur. On October 1, I was a CEO with an underwriting model.

That difference matters.

What Changes the Day After You Sell

Entrepreneurs wake up with a vision and bulldoze anything in the way. CEO of a PE-backed platform is a different role. You are executing a plan that a group of very smart, very analytical people underwrote. You have board meetings. You have targets that cascade into budgets, hiring plans, site pipelines, and weekly dashboards. None of that is bad. It is simply a different game.

I was young. Early thirties. Plenty of energy and belief. I wanted to keep driving. My self-awareness had not caught up to the new requirements. I still saw myself as the founder who could will things into existence. PE saw a portfolio company that needed to run the playbook. We did not converge fast enough. A year later, I was replaced.

At the time, it felt like getting kicked in the face. With distance, it is one of the best things that happened to me. It forced me to examine what I am good at, what I want, and how I should structure deals in the future.

Rolling Equity, Control, and the "49 Or 99" Lesson

Here is one lesson I wish I had learned sooner. If you are going to give up control, consider giving up almost all of it. Or keep real control. Do not live in the middle.

I sold 60 percent. That gave my partner control but left me with real skin in the game and a minority vote. I rolled a lot because I believed. There is nothing wrong with belief. In hindsight, I would either have sold 49 percent and kept control with a clear governance structure, or I would have sold 99 percent and moved on cleanly. Straddling the line meant I felt responsible but did not actually control the steering wheel.

That single choice drives a lot of downstream emotion. Be precise about what you want your work life to look like after close. Then structure the cap table and the governance to match that reality.

What PE Really Optimizes For

When you sell to PE, remember how their engine works. They get paid to deploy capital. They need to write sizable checks to businesses that can absorb that capital and grow. In restaurant and retail, that often means unit growth at speed.

Knowing this helps you put your own deal in perspective. If your business cannot take a lot of capital and convert it into growth, you will either be sized out or forced into a shape that does not fit you.

Life after Protein Bar

I crossed the table. Today I buy companies, usually from retiring owner-operators. I like situations that are not quite "ready for private equity." They are wonderful businesses with quirks that scare off financial buyers. A hand-coded ERP. A founder who still takes the biggest customer calls. A P&L printed from a system only three people on the planet can run. I buy them, fix the fragility, expand the commercial reach, and standardize the guts so the next buyer can underwrite the story in their language.

Here is the playbook I run.

1) Build anti-fragility

Most small companies are fragile for predictable reasons.

- **Single points of failure.** The owner holds the key vendor relationship, approves pricing, and covers the night shift when someone calls in sick. That is not a business. That is a hero act.

- **Aging infrastructure.** I own a livestock feed mill. It is a great company that throws off a million dollars a year in profit. The plant is fifty-plus years old. Something breaks all the time. You cannot sell "hope the auger holds" to a lender or a buyer.

- **Tribal systems.** The previous owner built a beautiful Unix system in the 1980s. It works flawlessly. No institutional buyer wants to bet on the only four humans who can run it.

To fix fragility, I spread relationships, put real managers in real seats, document the operating rhythm, address the critical maintenance, and migrate the financial and operating systems to something a buyer actually recognizes. NetSuite, QuickBooks, a sensible ERP. Precision beats romance.

2) Expand the commercial reach

Almost every seller has a list of growth ideas they never pursued. New channel. New product. New territory. Partnership with a complementary brand. When I ask why they did not do it, the answers are honest. "I did not have to." "I was tired." "I knew I would sell."

I push those second-generation growth levers. In the feed mill, it is brand and story. In other companies, it has been e-commerce overlays, wholesale programs, or pricing architecture. This is not a whiz-bang innovation theater. It is disciplined commercial stretch that a buyer can see, underwrite, and extrapolate.

3) Standardize how value is measured

If your reports require a decoder ring, you will restrict your buyer universe. Clean monthly closes. Accrual accounting. A simple KPI tree that rolls up into a forecast you hit more often than you miss. This is the boring work that creates exciting exits. The goal is to translate your excellence into a language lenders and investors speak fluently.

What Sellers Actually Want

Now that I buy companies, my opinion matters less than you might think. The seller's goals run the process. My job is to listen, respond honestly, and walk if we cannot agree.

Most deals fail on price. That is fine. I tell owners, "I am not saying your business is not worth ten million. I am saying I am not the buyer at that number." Clarity keeps friendships alive and options open.

When we do agree, the pattern is usually the same. Retiring owners want speed, certainty, and maximum cash at close. Entrepreneurs who still have fire sometimes want to keep a slice and chase a second bite later. Both approaches work. What does not work is pretending you want one when you feel the other.

I no longer want to partner in the middle. If I am giving up control as a seller, I look for clean deals that close fast with strong cash at close. Then I go build the next thing. That is my wiring. Yours might be different. Own it.

What I Would Tell My Younger Self on the Eve of that First Sale

- ➡ **Be explicit about your role post-close.** Do you want to be the visionary founder who hands the keys to a professional CEO and moves to a chairman role? Or do you want to be the operator who learns to live inside an underwriting model? Either can work. Both require different habits.

- ➡ **Decide your equity philosophy before you negotiate.** Control or clean exit. Forty-nine or ninety-nine. The middle is where regret lives.

- ➡ **Know the difference between a great PE firm and the right one for you.** I picked the most credible partner in my category. That was smart. I also should have tested harder for fit at the board level, alignment on pace, and agreement on what "good" looked like at 12, 24, and 36 months. Take references not just on deals that worked. Talk to founders whose deals did not work. Listen to how disagreements were handled.

- ➡ **Bring a real banker in early.** I asked North Point to help once I had a term sheet. They were excellent. If I did it again, I would still choose a relationship first, then let the banker run the process end to end. Competition sharpens outcomes. Good bankers also buffer emotions when things get tense.

➡ **Remember how PE math works.** You are not a precious snowflake. You are a line in a portfolio. That is not cynical. It is liberating. If you understand their incentives, you can negotiate a structure that respects theirs and protects yours.

A Note for Younger Founders with Juice in the Tank

A lot of owner-operators who read this will be younger. You built something real. You see ten more years in front of you. You also feel the tug to "take some chips off." That tension is normal.

Start with self-awareness. If you want to keep building, set up the company so the day to day does not depend on you. Put a president or COO in the seat for 12 to 24 months before you run a process. Move your key relationships to the org, not your phone. Prove the business can run if you take a two-week vacation and no one notices. That is how you earn both a higher multiple and more choices.

If you are ready to hand it off, hand it off. Do not sell 60 percent and tell yourself you still run the place. You will not. Sell most and move on. Or keep control and hire the people who make you unnecessary.

Timing the Market

When should you sell? My rule now is simple. Pay close attention to the first credible inbound inquiry. Not the generic "we are consolidating your space" email from an associate. The real one. The partner who flies in because they have a thesis, and you fit it. That is a leading indicator that other smart people are circling the same idea. That is often the right moment to decide if you want to be the hot girl at the dance again.

Why I Still Love this Game

Getting fired from the company I founded did not sour me on private equity or on selling. It taught me to be honest. Honest about who I am, what I want, and how to structure deals so the incentives line up. It also made me a better buyer. I can sit with an owner and talk about hiring, payroll, customer complaints, and what it feels like when the bank balance looks light on the 28th. Operators hear that and relax. We speak the same language.

The truth is simple. There are many good outcomes. You get to choose yours. Choose with clear eyes. Build a company that does not depend on your heroics. Tell your story in numbers that outsiders trust. Decide your role and your equity before you start the dance. And when the right partner shows up with a clear thesis and a real check, you will be ready to step onto the floor on your terms.

The Day We Said No—and What Changed After

Troy Kent, CEO, Kent Power

The worst time to learn what buyers care about is when they're asking you for it.

In 2019, we hired a banker, opened the books, and ran a full sale process. Diligence started at the same time as COVID lockdowns began. Eight months later, we walked away from a discounted offer. Not because we love drama. But because the number on the page reflected what our business looked like through a buyer's eyes: too much project work, not enough recurring contracts, over-concentrated customers, and numbers that took a spreadsheet marathon to produce. They weren't wrong. We just weren't ready.

Our "no" turned out to be the most valuable decision we've made in three generations.

I lead a utility construction company. We build and maintain power lines, natural gas lines, and electrical substations for investor-owned utilities, co-ops, and municipals. When a storm knocks out power, we roll. When a system needs a rebuild, we're there. Third generation. Great teams. Deep field roots. Proud of the work.

I was introduced to Seth through our strategy coach. We clicked because his core message is blunt and useful: see your company the way a buyer would, then build it that way, whether you sell or not. I didn't fully get it until I lived it.

How A "Pretty Good" Business Turns into a Discounted Offer

Here's what happened.

We went to market heavy on lumpier, one-off projects. Engineers at our customers went home during COVID, new jobs slowed, and our backlog began to burn off. We were busy answering diligence requests—every one of them a manual data pull—while the core business needed attention. By the time we reached the finish line, our visibility had narrowed, and the price reflected that risk. We declined. It stung. It was also a wake-up call.

Coming home from that last meeting, I started reading everything I could on M&A and private equity. It felt like reading a script after playing the part. Good cop, bad cop, timeline pressure, "last and best"— it was all there. The lesson wasn't that we'd been played. The lesson was that we had asked the market to value the business we *wished* we had, not the one we *actually* ran.

If it's important to a buyer, it ought to be important to the owner.

The Rebuild: Turning the Buyer's Checklist into Our Operating Plan

We took the punch and then got to work. No speeches—just changes.

1) Add ballast to the model.

We set a target mix between projects and recurring revenue and began pursuing longer-term MSAs and term work. Not glamorous, incredibly stabilizing. When you're in our world, visibility matters as much as velocity.

2) Diversify customers and work types.

Concentration had crept up because a few big names were outspending everyone else. That's a double-edged sword. We pushed for breadth—new customers, new geographies, and adjacent scopes—so no single decision could swing a quarter.

3) Make numbers fast, clean, and boring.

During diligence, we discovered how much we were relying on heroics. We upgraded systems so the core reports are push-button: backlog coverage, MSA run-rate, mix by customer, WIP, cash conversion, safety and productivity metrics. The goal is not to impress anyone with a fancy model. The goal is to know the business in real time.

4) Protect the backlog while you sell—or while you sleep.

We built a rhythm for renewing work and filling the pipe that does not depend on me personally returning every phone call. Sales has a cadence. Ops has a cadence. Finance closes on time. If we ever run a process again, the company will keep operating like nothing's happening.

5) Invest in people—and in myself.

I came up through the field. After that failed process, I owned the gaps. I learned the financial side hard and fast, so I could ask better questions and make better decisions. We adjusted our org design so team structure supports scale instead of capping it. No blame, just evolution.

What changed? Just about everything. We've nearly doubled since that first run at a sale—and we're in a healthier position across the board. The point isn't the headline number. It's that the business is less fragile and more valuable whether we transact or not.

What We'd Do Differently Next Time

I don't know exactly when—or even whether—we'll sell. Growth finances itself until it doesn't, and our customers can be slow payers in tough periods. We might entertain a partner to support the next leg. If we do, here's how we'll run it:

- → **Build the data room before the first meeting.** Not just folders. Reconciled, recurring reports that tie to the general ledger and to the field reality.

- → **Name a strike team.** A small cross-functional group handles all requests. Everyone else keeps serving customers. Protect the backlog like it's oxygen.

- → **Set the guardrails.** What mix of cash, earnout, and rollover we'd accept. What we want the transition to look like. Where we're flexible and where we're not.

→ **Demand fit, not just price.** Utilities are long-term relationships. Safety culture is non-negotiable. If a buyer doesn't respect that, the check won't make it better.

→ **Keep running the business.** Hit the plan. Over-deliver in the window when they're watching. No surprises.

I would go into any potential future process with 98 percent of what a buyer needs already on the table and the discipline to say yes or no quickly.

Platform Ambitions, With Humility

Could we be a platform? That's the direction we're building toward. We've made one small acquisition before—and we did it poorly. Honest truth. The valuation was fuzzy, the integration was fuzzier. It taught us what *not* to do.

With Seth, we're doing the groundwork the right way: building a "filter and funnel"—who we target, where we create value for them, and how we integrate them cleanly. Clear selection criteria. Integration playbooks. Cultural fit first. No more hoping it works out after the close.

If the right opportunity shows up, I'd like us to be the company that others want to join, not the one that simply pays the most.

Keeping options open—for the business and the family

I've got three sons, twenty to twenty-nine. Maybe they'll come into the business. Maybe they won't. My job is to build something healthy enough that they have a real choice. That means two parallel tracks:

→ **Grow as if we'll own it forever.** Safer, stronger, steadier. Systems that outlive the founder.

→ **Prepare as if we'll sell in a few years.** Clean financials, diversified demand, documented processes, credible second bench.

Best of Both Worlds. Real Optionality.

What I tell owners who are where I was

You might be a lot like us in 2019—successful by most measures, busy as ever, and about to invite a dozen smart people to evaluate the only company you've ever run. It's tempting to let the deal team set the agenda. Don't. Set your own.

- ➡ **Don't take your eye off the ball.** The company must perform while you process. Assign a small team to defend the front door; everyone else stays on the field.

- ➡ **Turn manual into measurable.** If a data request takes three days and four people, you don't *know* your business yet—you're reconstructing it.

- ➡ **Balance the book.** If your revenue is 90 percent projects, get serious about recurring. Buyers will price that risk. So will a storm.

- ➡ **Spread the risk.** Customer concentration is fun until it isn't. Build breadth on purpose.

- ➡ **Invest in your own learning.** If you came up through the trade, get dangerous on the finance side. If you came up through finance, spend more time with the crews. Your questions get better, and so do outcomes.

- ➡ **Be ready to say no.** The power to decline only exists if you're building a better version of the business while the process runs.

I can't say we enjoyed having eight-plus months end in a pass. But I can say the direction we're headed today was defined there. We added ballast. We diversified. We made our numbers boring and our operations calmer. We focused on increasing cash flow. We doubled. More importantly, we grew up.

Because that's the point. Build a company the market loves to buy and you'll love to own. If you end up selling, great. If you don't, you'll be running a safer, stronger business with more sleep at night.

The worst time to learn what buyers care about is while they're asking you for it. We learned the hard way. You don't have to. Start now.

PART IV: THE DEAL

CHAPTER 11

QUALITY OF DEAL STRUCTURE

When the dust settles, the deal structure is the final verdict. It's the scoreboard. It's how private equity says, "Here's what we believe about your business and your future."

And here's the part most founders don't realize: the deal structure is *not* just about valuation. It's a mirror reflecting your business as seen from the outsider's perspective.

Through the deal structure, investors are valuing/concluding on three things:

1. Is this business transactable?

2. What are we willing to pay?

3. And under what structure are we willing to do the deal? That is, how much risk are we willing to take?

What That Headline Number Really Means

Let's talk about the money.

When people hear a business sold for $20 million, it sounds like a huge win—and it *is*. But the founder doesn't walk away with $20 million.

There are several things that come out of that top-line number—many of which are poorly understood by first-time sellers:

➡ **Transaction fees** (investment banker, legal, accounting, etc.)

➡ **Taxes**, which vary widely based on structure, timing, and jurisdiction

➡ **Working capital requirements**, meaning a portion of the company's cash and receivables, typically stays in the business

➡ **Indemnification and escrow holdbacks**, where a portion of the proceeds is set aside for a defined period in case of any post-closing liabilities

➡ **Rollover equity**, if applicable, where you reinvest part of your proceeds into the new company

In the end, that $20 million headline sale might translate to $10–12 million in actual cash proceeds after taxes and fees—possibly less if the deal includes a large rollover or earnout.

It's still life-changing money. But it's rarely as clean or immediate as most sellers expect.

The takeaway here is simple: **start preparing now.** Talk to professionals. Get clarity on what different deal structures mean. Understand your tax exposure and liquidity options. Think deeply about what you want your life to look like—after the business is no longer yours.

Because if you're well-prepared—mentally, emotionally, and financially—you'll not only sell smarter, you'll *live better* after the sale.

Founder Intent Drives Structure

Every founder brings his or her own goals to the table. Some want to retire and ride off with as much cash as possible. Others want to stay on and scale with a larger platform. Some are seeking one last growth chapter before handing over the reins.

These motivations shape the deal just as much as EBITDA or gross margin. A founder who wants to roll equity and be part of a larger play will likely accept different terms than one who wants to sell outright. And buyers structure accordingly—aligning incentives, limiting risk, and ensuring that the business's readiness matches the founder's.

The Market Sets a Range—Structure Closes the Gap

Founders tend to anchor on the highest multiple they've heard from a friend or read online. "My buddy sold for 10x EBITDA." But does your business look like theirs?

Let's take a commercial HVAC business doing $20–50M in revenue. Some firms in t hat range e arn 8 % EBITDA, o thers 14%. S ome have recurring maintenance revenue; others are entirely project-based. Some are union shops, others aren't. Each of those dimensions affects both valuation and structure.

That's how you end up with one business trading at 4x and another at 10x.

The gap between *aspiration* and *achievement* is bridged through deal structure.

Let's look at some real-world examples.

Case 1: Add-On with Performance Variability

Say you're a founder of a $15M revenue HVAC business with 10% EBITDA margins. You've had a great year or two, but prior performance was a little lumpy. A PE-backed platform wants to acquire you as an add-on.

Here's a structure you might be offered:

➡ **Valuation:** 5x EBITDA

➡ **Structure:**

- One-third cash at close

- One-third in a three-year earnout tied to revenue growth and margin stability
- One-third rollover equity into the holding company

You walk away with some liquidity, but you're also tied to the performance of the business post-sale—and to the success of the broader platform. If things go well, that rollover might generate a strong second exit. If not, it's at risk.

PE structures the deal this way because they need you to stay involved. They see promise—but they want you to prove it.

Case 2: Strong Platform Candidate

Now imagine a $40M HVAC business with 12% EBITDA and 70% of revenue from long-term maintenance contracts. Predictable cash flow, sound systems, and a clear succession plan.

This is a very different story.

➡ **Valuation:** 6x EBITDA

➡ **Structure:**

- 70% cash at close
- 30% rollover equity
- No earnout

Why no earnout? Because the numbers—and the leadership—are already strong. The buyer has confidence in future performance.

Case 3: Retiring Founder, Succession Risk

Let's say a founder wants to retire immediately—but the successor is unproven. Maybe there's a good #2 in place, but that person hasn't led solo yet. That's risk.

In a case like this, the deal might look like:

➡ **Valuation:** 5.5x

➡ **Structure:**

- 60% cash

- 20% rollover equity

- 20% earnout over two years, tied to successor team performance

This forces alignment. It puts real dollars behind the founder's claim that "my team can run this without me." It also gives PE some downside protection if that turns out not to be true.

Case 4: The Rare All-Cash Exit

All-cash deals still happen—but not often. Maybe 10–15% of the time. Usually only when:

➡ The business is a clear standout in its space

➡ There's proven management already running it

➡ The founder has already stepped back operationally

In those cases, a buyer may be willing to go all-cash at close. But even then, it's not the norm. PE doesn't have hard collateral to backstop the deal—they're not buying buildings or machinery. They're buying cash flow. And that makes them cautious.

Why Skin in the Game Matters

Here's what PE really wants: shared risk, shared upside.

They want you to have some skin in the game—whether that's in the form of rollover equity, an earnout, or both. They are asking you to bet on the future of the business with them.

Rollover equity is often the cleanest path. It's tax-deferred, and if things go well, you can continue to invest in future 'upside' in other transactions down the road.

But not all founders like it. Some want to be out, emotionally and financially. That's fine—but if that's your posture, expect a haircut. If the business still needs you post-close and you're not willing to roll or earn it out, PE will price in that risk.

Deal Structure Tells the Truth

Deal structure is the real worth of a business. It tells you how buyers *really* view your company.

- If you get 80% cash and no earnout, they trust the fundamentals.
- If half your proceeds are tied to future performance, they don't.
- If they insist on rollover, they want alignment—or they're worried you're irreplaceable.

Deal structure is not just the last chapter of the deal—it's the summary of the whole book.

It reflects your leadership. Your financial systems. Your recurring revenue. Your team. Your readiness.

You don't get to negotiate your way around those facts. You only get to prove them—or not.

What Founders Should Take Away

If you want optionality—whether that's a complete exit, a partial exit, or a strategic partnership with real upside—start with the fundamentals.

Get the financials tight and the reporting timely. Build the team. Drive recurring revenue. Set up systems that don't rely on your daily involvement.

Because in the end, the deal you get is the story you've already written.

And structure is how private equity decides whether they believe it.

Understanding the Deal Timeline

Once you decide that a sale may be in your future—whether that's six months out or five years down the road—it's time to start thinking seriously about the timeline and what it takes to navigate it well. This isn't just about the logistics of getting to a close. It's about whether you're emotionally and strategically prepared for what comes next.

You've built something meaningful. But eventually, every owner hits a point where they want—or need—to turn that value into liquidity. For some, that's retirement. For others, it's burnout, or a desire to take risk off the table. Others see opportunity ahead and want a capital partner to help unlock it. There's no right answer—only your desired outcome. But whatever your reason, clarity matters. If you don't know why you're selling, it's hard to make the right decisions when deal terms get real.

Roughly 200,000 small businesses will sell each year in the U.S. Only about 35% of those will go to third parties—like private equity, family offices, or strategics. This book focuses on that subset. And what distinguishes those deals from the others is the rigor. Third-party sales are more demanding, more structured, and more financially driven. If you're going that route, it's not enough to have a good business. You must prove its long-term sustainability.

This is where the concept of the valuation gap becomes critical. At any given moment, your business is worth what the market is willing to pay for it as-is. But that number can change dramatically depending on how investor-ready your company is. If you've been following along with this book, you've seen how issues like financial reporting, leadership bench, client concentration, and margin quality all impact deal structure and valuation. Most of those factors are within your control—if you give yourself the time to address them before going to market.

So, the deal timeline isn't just about getting a transaction done. It's about using the time you have to shift the leverage in your favor. The more buttoned-up you are, the better your outcome will be—both in terms of valuation and in the terms you're offered.

As you begin to consider a transaction, you'd be well served to find someone you trust who understand transactions in your industry and get a real sense of how the market might see you, how the deal might be structured, and what value range you'd likely land in. Compare that against your own expectations. You may still choose to move forward. You may not. But at least you'll be moving forward on purpose—with eyes wide open.

What the Sale Timeline *Actually* Looks Like

Let's say you're ready. You want to go to market, and you're planning to hire a banker or intermediary to run the process. That timeline breaks into three phases:

1. **Preparation (2–3 months):** This is when you're building the materials—financials, story, forecast, and more. If you've done the work already (clean books, clear KPIs, leadership bench), this goes faster. If not, this is where the scrambling begins. Better to do this prep in advance, even if you're still 1–2 years out.

2. **Buyer Process (2–3 months):** Once you hit the market, it takes time to gather interest, field questions, and collect preliminary offers or term sheets. This is your "buyer pool" phase—akin to getting multiple offers on a house.

3. **Exclusivity to Close (3–4 months):** Once you choose a buyer and sign an LOI, the diligence clock starts. LOIs are non-binding, and in the lower middle market, only about one in three actually close. Why? Surprises in diligence. Shifting priorities. Poor preparation. Again— get ready before you start.

Altogether, that's roughly 8–10 months from launch to close in a typical banker-led process. It can go faster, but only when prep work has already been done.

If you're not going to market but still get an inbound call and start responding, the timeline compresses slightly. You might share financials for a month or two, get a term sheet, and then enter the 3–4 month diligence phase. But even then, it's a five-to-six-month journey, minimum.

Competitive Tension, Certainty, and Closing

Whether you run a process or take a proprietary offer, one fact holds: deals are risky until they close. That's why many experienced sellers prefer to work with a banker. A banker brings competitive tension, which forces buyers to sharpen their pencils. And a good banker knows how to spot a serious buyer from one who's just fishing.

Still, there are plenty of founders who sell *without* a banker—especially if they're joining a friend's platform, or have a personal relationship with a private equity sponsor. These "warm" deals can move faster, but they still carry the same risks: no deal is done until it's signed, funded, and closed.

So, whatever your path, go in with clarity. Understand what a real timeline looks like. Know how long you need to prepare, how long it takes to run a process, and how long diligence can drag on. And most of all, start with the internal work. Be honest with yourself about your readiness, expectations, and goals. That's the part that takes the longest—and pays off the most.

Building, Selling, and Staying On: What I Learned Taking a Home Services Company to a Premium Exit

Jim Probst, President, SBE Odyssey

Selling a company isn't a miracle moment—it's the culmination of years of boring, disciplined execution punctuated by a handful of hard decisions you can't afford to get wrong. I've lived both lives: the first half of my career in high-growth, venture-backed operating roles (even took a company public in the '90s); the second half building a home services business with my brother, growing it from a money-loser to a market leader and ultimately selling it to a private equity platform for a premium multiple. I then stayed on for two and a half years to deliver the earnout, transition leadership, and make sure the machine kept running.

If you're reading this because you're thinking about selling to private equity, here's the through-line: execution beats everything, culture fit is not optional, and you need a plan—down to the who, when, and how—for the day after close.

From "Nice Little Business" to a Real Platform

We started Quality Home Maintenance with a simple thesis: out-train, out-execute, out-last. In 2009, we acquired the George Brazil HVAC brand. At the time, the company did roughly $2 million in revenue and was losing about $500,000 a year. Thirteen years later, by the time we sold on June 30, 2022, we were at roughly $48 million in revenue and healthy profitability. We rang about 70,000 doorbells a year and had about 250 employees in the field and office.

The deal we closed reflected the work: a premium multiple—12.5x —with cash at close and a meaningful two-year earnout layered on top. No rollover equity. That last part wasn't an accident; it was a choice. I'll come back to why that mattered.

The First Trip to Market—and the Wake-Up Call

We first went to market in the fall of 2019. I'd run sale processes before and thought I could self-manage it. Within weeks, the market gave me feedback I couldn't ignore.

Every serious buyer we met already owned assets in our category. They knew exactly what "great" looked like—growth rates, margins, call-through rates, technician productivity, close rates, you name it. They politely told us their portfolio comps were performing above our levels. Translation: we were comfortable, not optimized.

That was the wake-up call. We paused the process, went back to work, and made execution the obsession. Training—already a strength—became a system. We ran technicians, salespeople, and leaders through a cadence of coaching we'd never attempted. Over the next stretch, we added roughly $10 million of revenue, with earnings to match. Same market. Same brand. Same team. Different level of execution.

If you want a premium valuation, don't argue with the market. Listen to it, tune your machine, and come back with proof.

Culture Fit Is a Deal Term

When we re-engaged the market, interest flooded in. I'm rounding, but we had 20–25 serious groups leaning in and wound up with low-20s LOIs. We narrowed the field and went deep with one buyer. Terms were strong. Everyone was excited. Then, two to three weeks before close, it didn't feel right.

I had been clear with every suitor from day one: I value the number and the cultural fit equally. Not "almost equally." Equally. We had 250 teammates and a brand we'd built brick by brick. If we were going to hand them to someone, we needed alignment on how people are trained, how performance is measured, and how customers are treated. As we neared the finish line with that first buyer, our views of the future diverged. We went pencils down.

That's a terrifying sentence if you need the deal. We didn't. The business was healthy. The market was hot. And our values weren't negotiable. Days later, Ashish—the founder of NearU—called. Our first conversation was about training and workforce development. It sounded like we'd written the same playbook. We signed a new LOI, moved through diligence, and closed roughly four to five months later. Right buyer, right terms, right fit.

If you take nothing else from this: treat culture as a headline term. The wrong partner at the right price will cost you more than you can imagine.

The Deal We Chose: All Cash + Earnout, No Rollover

Most platforms today expect sellers to roll 20–30% of proceeds into holdco (holding company) equity. Doing so aligns interests and conserves their cash. We went a different route: cash at close and a two-year earnout on top, structured simply—hit incremental earnings targets, get paid a defined multiple of the outperformance.

Why? Clarity. Our partnership group had five people—three primary shareholders at ~30% each and two at ~5%—with different ages, timelines, and appetites for the next ride. We wanted a clean result with upside for continued outperformance during a defined period. The earnout did exactly what it's supposed to do: kept us engaged and focused, without creating ambiguity about who owned what and for how long.

There's no "right" answer here—rollover can be fantastic. But know what you want before you go to market and be prepared to defend it. If you're fuzzy, you'll get talked into someone else's plan.

Staying on Without Staying Stuck

Staying post-close can be a dream or a slog. Mine worked because we set it up that way. Day one, I had a COO ready to step into the top seat once my two-year commitment ended. We purposely gave him two full peak seasons to learn the business under pressure before I stepped aside. We officially hit my end date on June 30th, but you don't abandon an HVAC business mid-summer; my leadership team and I stayed through year-end to hand off cleanly.

Crucially, I didn't wear "two hats." My job was the same as before: drive growth and execution at George Brazil. Yes, as part of a larger portfolio (NearU had 20-plus companies), there are portfolio-level rhythms—reporting, accountability, shared services. But because of my earlier corporate background, none of that spooked me. I knew what would help, what would distract, and I was willing to push back on mandates that didn't fit our business while embracing those that did. Respectful friction is part of being a good portfolio citizen.

The Three-Year Arc That Mattered

People love to talk about "the process." Here's the real arc:

➡ **Year 1:** Go to market (2019), listen to the feedback, realize we're not where the premium comps are, pull the listing.

➡ **Year 2:** Fix it. Train harder. Tighten ops. Add ~$10M revenue. Lift earnings. Build the bench. Make the business *obviously* better.

➡ **Year 3:** Re-enter (2022), choose the right buyer, negotiate a deal that matches our goals, close, and then execute again under the new banner.

Could we have sold earlier? Sure. Would we have gotten 12.5x and the terms we wanted? Unlikely. The difference wasn't a new story; it was a new performance.

Hire the Banker Who Actually Knows Your Space

I tried to run the 2019 process myself. It had been twenty years since my last go-round. The landscape had changed—data rooms, buyer sophistication, legal complexity, and the speed of diligence. When we went back out, we hired the premier banker for home services. It was night and day. They ran a real process, brought the right buyers, absorbed a massive amount of the transactional work, and let us keep the main thing the main thing: performance.

If you're doing sub-$10M revenue and marginal profit, you may not get attention from top shops; you might need to bootstrap your way to bankable scale first. But once you're in the fairway, the right banker is worth every penny—especially if you intend to *overperform* during the process (you should).

Execution is the Multiplier

Everyone wants the three things investors pay for: growth, margins, and management. You don't talk your way into those. You operate your way into them.

For us, that meant:

➡ **Training as a system.** We were a training company disguised as a contractor. Techs, sales, dispatch, managers—everyone had a curriculum, coaching cadence, and defined KPIs. Training wasn't an event; it was oxygen.

➡ **Daily accountability.** Scoreboards, ride-alongs, call reviews, close-rate ladders, conversion funnels. Everyone knew the number that mattered for their seat and how today's activity created tomorrow's revenue.

➡ **Leadership bench.** Succession wasn't a slide in a deck. It was a named person with a start date, responsibilities, and authority, onboarded two years before I exited.

➡ **Non-negotiable service standards.** Brand is behavior. You don't earn 70,000 doorbells a year without consistent experience at the customer's home.

None of this is sexy. All of it is bankable.

Treat Performance during Diligence as Life-or-Death

The single biggest unforced error I see: sellers let performance slip while the deal is in flight. Diligence is a second job—12 workstreams, hundreds of requests, weekly buyer calls, lawyers drafting reps and warranties at midnight. If you don't shield your operators, the machine seizes up right when buyers are deciding whether to stretch, retrade, or walk.

We avoided that by design. My Director of Operations took point on diligence. There was almost nothing she didn't know about our business, so she could service requests quickly while I and the rest of the team protected field performance. The rule was simple: *we can't miss*. Buyers love momentum; they penalize stumbles. Keep the scoreboard green.

Know Where You Won't Bend

Private equity platforms have playbooks—shared services, procurement standards, reporting formats, tech stacks. Many of those bring real benefit. Some don't fit your operation. You need the judgment and backbone to tell the difference.

My posture post-close was straightforward: if a change helped us serve customers better, grow faster, or improve control, we embraced it. If it threatened our standards or time-to-serve, we debated it hard. That wasn't rebellion; it was stewardship. Interestingly, the more clearly we argued from data and outcomes, the more respect we earned. You sold because you built something that works—don't abandon the reasons it works.

Why We Didn't Take Rollover Equity

A lot of friends asked why we didn't "double-dip." After all, rollover equity can produce another bite at the apple when the platform sells again. Three reasons:

1. **Shareholder alignment.** With five owners at different stages of life, "clean now" beat "maybe later."

2. **Control of time.** The earnout was a defined window with a defined formula. No ambiguity about when we were done.

3. **Clarity of focus.** Our mission post-close was singular: exceed the plan and hand off a self-sustaining business. No split attention between our old business and a new holdco cap table.

Again: not a moral stance. Just alignment between structure and goals. Decide *your* goals early.

The Questions You Need to Answer Before You Start

The worst time to figure out who you are and what you want is while term sheets are flying. Do this work now:

➡ **What, exactly, are you selling?** A job that depends on you, or a system that runs without you?

➡ **What's your non-negotiable?** Is culture equal to price, or not? Write it down.

➡ **Cash, rollover, earnout—what mix fits your life?** There's no perfect structure. There is a perfect structure for *you*.

➡ **Who replaces you, and when?** Names, dates, onboarding plan. Not ideas.

➡ **Can you keep performance *up* while diligence runs?** Who is point on requests? What gets deprioritized? What metrics must not dip?

If you can't answer those, you're not ready.

What I'd Do Differently

People ask me this and expect a gotcha. Honestly, not much. We made plenty of small mistakes—as everyone does—but the big calls were right: pausing after the first market test, investing in training, refusing the wrong cultural fit even with a great number on the table, choosing a structure that matched our goals, hiring the right banker, protecting performance, and preparing a real successor. Most of all, we never compromised our values to "get it done." Money doesn't fix that kind of mistake; it exposes it.

Parting Advice for Owner-Operators

➡ **Execution is the story.** If buyers' comps outperform you today, don't argue—upgrade. Add the $10 million before you ask them to pay for it.

➡ **Culture is a term, not a talking point.** Treat it with the same seriousness as price and reps & warranties.

➡ **Pick your structure on purpose.** Rollover is powerful. So is clean cash and a clear earnout. Choose what fits your shareholders and season of life.

➡ **Build the bench early.** A successor hired *after* close is a risk. A successor hired *before* close is a reason to pay you more.

➡ **Protect performance like oxygen.** Assign a diligence quarterback who can live in the data room so the field doesn't miss a beat.

➡ **Hire the banker who lives your industry.** They'll bring the right buyers and absorb the drag so you can keep winning while the process runs.

We sold a business we were proud of to a buyer we respected, on terms that matched our goals. Then we did the hard part: we kept winning after the champagne. If that's the outcome you want, start now. Train harder. Measure tighter. Decide what you won't compromise. And when the right buyer shows up, you'll be ready—not just to close, but to hand them a machine that runs. That's how you earn your valuation.

How Law Firm Owners Actually Get Paid

By Tom Lenfestey, CEO, The Law Practice Exchange

If you own a law firm, you are sitting on an asset you probably cannot see. Most lawyers treat their firm like a job with overhead. I treat it like a business with value. My work is helping you turn the thing you built into the freedom you want—all on your own terms.

I am an attorney and a CPA who moved into the intermediary world about fifteen years ago. My lane is narrow on purpose. I live in the legal niche all day. I advise sellers, run processes, and, when needed, sit shoulder to shoulder with owners for months to get the firms ready to sell. Arizona's 2021 rule changes allowing for non-attorneys to own practices did not create my mission, but they accelerated it. So did the rise of private equity interest, LSOs, and better tech.

The short version is simple. You now have options. Your job is to make your firm ready so those options are real, allowing you to exit on your own terms before life makes those decisions for you.

Build to Exit, Even If You Never Sell

The best time to think about a sale is the day you open your doors. That mindset does not make you greedy—it makes you disciplined. What drives exit value also drives better margins and a calmer life while you still own the firm.

The Three Levers Buyers Pay For

I coach every owner to focus on three levers. Push these and your multiple moves. Ignore them, and you will live with discounts and structure that won't give you the peace of mind you deserve.

1) Financials that are real and attractive

Buyers want clean books, accrual accounting, and a rhythm that closes on time. The higher your earnings and the cleaner the reporting, the larger the buyer pool.

If you want to move from a 4x world to an 8x world, grow revenue, widen margins, and be able to prove both with data that ties to your trust accounting and your GL. That sounds basic, but in our niche, this level of organization is still rare. The rarity is why the multiple moves when you get it right.

2) Uniqueness that is bigger than you

Buyers ask one quiet question: "How hard would this be to copy?" If your answer is "not very," the price falls.

This is where brand matters. I want your **firm brand** to be the draw, not only your last name. Invest in the position, the promise, and the proof. Show a repeatable way you bring clients in and move them to an outcome. Build a moat that looks like a reputation, a specialization, a referral flywheel, a content engine, or a digital funnel that actually converts. The more your demand engine is the firm and not you, the less risky you are and the better your terms look to potential buyers.

3) Systems that run without you

This is the law firm problem. For decades, it was the norm for owners to do everything. Intake. Strategy. Court. Payroll. Marketing. With that model, you will still sell, but your check will be light and your earnout will be heavy.

Invest in people and processes so the work moves through the firm without you as the bottleneck. Document the way you practice. Measure it. Hold people to it. If you can take a two-week vacation and billing does not dip, your value just went up.

Timing and Process

Owners often ask, "When should I start?" My answer is *now*. The best outcomes I see come from owners who start the conversation two to four years before they plan to transact. They meet prospective partners. They learn what the market rewards. They tune the firm. They build trust.

Could you start six months before you want to retire? Yes. You will get a result. It just may not be the result you wanted.

Our typical path looks like this:

1. **Baseline valuation.** Current value, buyer universe, likely structures.

2. **Gap plan.** Specific projects in finance, brand, and systems to lift value.

3. **Light market engagement.** Warm introductions, not a blast. Pattern recognition begins.

4. **Run the firm.** Hit numbers while you improve the machine.

5. **Full process.** When the story and numbers align, we go.

Through all of it, keep your eye on performance. Many deals stumble because the owner takes their eye off the ball during a process. Do less yourself. Empower your team so the firm keeps producing while you negotiate.

Two Quick Stories

The internal succession that wasn't.

A founder planned to sell to two long-time associates. He delayed, then delayed again. When he finally pushed, the associates told him they could not be partners. He was months from the date he had promised his family. Forty employees were looking to him for a plan.

We ran to the market with a tight story and a clear transition plan. We found a firm that valued his brand, wanted his team, and could absorb the admin load. He took a slightly lower headline price than another offer because the fit and the transition plan were better. Two days after closing, he sent a note that said, "I gave up control. I gained sleep." That is the trade many owners want but do not say out loud.

The thirty-something who built with intent.

Another client was in her thirties. Great numbers. A firm brand that pulled clients in. Systems that let her bill less and lead more. She was expecting her second child and wanted time at home. There was nothing broken— she simply wanted a different season of life.

We placed her with a buyer who valued what she had built and did not need her to hold the whole firm up. She took meaningful cash at close, a reasonable performance tail, and the freedom to choose her pace. Exits are not only for the sixty-five-year-old. They are for anyone who builds an asset and wants to monetize at the right time for their life.

How to Raise Your Multiple in the Next 12 to 24 Months

Here is the short punch list I give owners who want to create options fast.

- ➡ **Hire a real finance lead.** Close the books monthly and convert to accrual if you have not. Build a dashboard that ties intake to revenue and revenue to margin.

- ➡ **Own your demand.** Shift from personal referrals you control to firm channels you can teach. Digital, content, events, partnerships. You pick the mix and transform it into how the firm grows.

- ➡ **Document the practice.** Intake scripts. Case workflows. Quality checks. Deadlines. Build the playbook and use it.

- ➡ **Build the team.** Put accountable leaders in intake, operations, and finance. Give them numbers and let them answer questions in meetings.

- ➡ **Reduce key-person risk.** If you are the rainmaker and the trial lawyer and the person signing checks, you are the risk. Spread the load.

- ➡ **Talk to buyers early.** Not to sell tomorrow, but to learn what the best buyer for your firm values so you can build it.

Do these things to see your value rise and your options multiply. Most importantly, your life gets better even if you never sell.

What Success Feels Like

A great outcome does not feel like a magic trick. It feels like clarity. The owner knows their number. The buyer knows the plan. The transition is real. The staff sees a future. The clients get served. And the founder walks out of the building with something better than control. They walk out on terms they decided in advance.

You deserve that. You get there by building a firm that runs on numbers, brand, and systems. You get there by starting before you need to. You get there by picking partners for fit and plan, not only for price.

You do not have to do all of this alone. My job is to help you see the asset you already have, upgrade the parts that matter, and orchestrate the moment when you turn years of work into the next chapter of your life.

Your Next Three Moves

1. **Get a baseline valuation.** Get a number you're comfortable with from qualified valuation professionals so you know where you stand. If your value isn't where you want it, start by picking and fixing three things holding you back to get the ball rolling.

2. **Pick your twelve-month projects.** One finance, one brand, one system. Put an owner and a date on each.

3. **Start the conversations.** Meet real buyers. Learn. Build trust. Keep running the firm and hit your numbers while you network to find the right fit.

Options create leverage. Preparation creates options. If you build with exit in mind, you will enjoy the practice more today and you will get paid properly when it is time to hand the keys to the next owner.

CHAPTER 12

QUALITY OF POST-DEAL PREPARATION

Selling is an event. Living with the outcome is a phase. This chapter is about that phase—what the first year really feels like after you close, and how to prepare yourself and your team so the deal becomes a springboard, not a sinkhole.

The Three (Real) Post-Deal Paths

In this book, we're focused on third-party sales. For such transactions, most founders land in one of three buckets:

1. **Retire at close.** You sell and step off the field.

2. **Planned retirement.** You sell and agree to transition out over 18–36 months.

3. **Stay and build.** You sell and keep going—either as an add-on leader inside an existing platform or as the CEO of a newly created platform.

Each has a different level of post-deal responsibility, scrutiny, and change.

Changes to Plan For

Retiring right at close—or on a planned glidepath—creates a different kind of transition. Operationally, you'll be stepping back; psychologically, you'll be decelerating from 100 mph to something far slower. Think about that now, not after the wire clears.

Sketch the first 90 days after close: Where will you be? How will you spend mornings? What projects (business or personal) will absorb your drive? If you're staying for a defined transition, be explicit with the buyer about what you *will* own (knowledge transfer, key relationships, successor support) and what you *won't* (open-ended firefights). Plan the hand-offs and celebrate the team. The goal is a clean transfer, not a slow fade.

On the personal side, decide how involved you want to remain as an owner, mentor, or board observer—if at all. Align your investment policy statement with your new liquidity to avoid replacing operator anxiety with market anxiety. And if philanthropy, teaching, or angel investing are on your list, line up the first small commitments now; momentum matters.

The Seller's Hangover

No one prepares you for the emotional whiplash. Before the deal, you hadn't had a boss in years. After the deal you have owners, a board, lenders—and an employment agreement. You're still vital, but you're not *sovereign*.

There may be a mix of relief, fatigue, and "what did I just do?" You may forget that the investor backed *you* to grow the asset. They don't know your business as well as you do, but they will expect regular reporting, visibility, and accountability—quickly.

Some founders blast through this with fresh energy and no bumps. Most feel at least a wobble because a big part of their identity so far has been "entrepreneur" and "independent." You built something real. Monetizing it is an achievement, not an abdication. Keep that framing.

When doubt creeps in, reconnect to *why* you did the deal—liquidity, growth, de-risking, a bigger platform for your team—and keep it visible. I've seen founders put their "why" at the top of board decks for the first six months as a reminder to themselves as much as to their investors.

How to Prepare Yourself Before You Close

You can soften the landing if you do a few things *before* signing:

➤ **Rehearse the new reality.** Walk through a mock board pack. Practice a lender update. Get comfortable with a monthly KPI cadence now.

➤ **Protect recovery time.** Block at least a week post-close for rest and re-entry. Your team will need you to be clear-headed in weeks 2–6, not exhausted on day one.

➤ **Write the Day-1 memo.** Have your "what this means for us" message ready: purpose, priorities, goals, and a 100-day outline.

➤ **Name the core team.** Who runs integration? Who owns each VCP initiative? Who closes the books and owns lender reporting?

Post-deal preparation isn't about bracing for impact—it's about installing the scaffolding that lets you climb higher after the transaction.

Normal Reactions in the First 90 Days:

➤ A dip in energy after an intense sale process ("I've been working two jobs").

➤ Second-guessing or mild regret—even when the deal was good.

➤ Friction as you recalibrate from total control to shared governance.

None of this means the deal was wrong. It means you're human.

Why the First 6–9 Months Can Dip

During a sale, leadership attention splinters. A handful of people know what's going on; everyone else senses something and fills the gaps with stories. Right after close, that stored-up uncertainty becomes FUD—fear, uncertainty, doubt.

At the same time, you and the new owners are launching change: new reporting, new priorities, sometimes new leaders. It's common to see a short-term dip in performance as everyone adjusts and the company absorbs the transaction costs (literal and emotional).

Plan for it:

➡ **Over-communicate internally** in the first 30–60 days. What's the strategy? What's staying the same? What's changing and why?

➡ **Re-center the operating rhythm** (weekly reviews, customer pipeline, cash). Deals end. Operations continue.

➡ **Stage the to-do list.** Not everything needs to change in Q1.

Life with Investors and a Board

If you've never had outside owners, the first quarter will feel different:

➡ **Governance cadence.** Board meetings begin quickly. Expect a 100-day plan, monthly KPI packs, and a rhythm of pre-reads, meetings and follow-ups.

➡ **Value creation plan (VCP).** The board will align with you on 3–7 initiatives that move the needle (pricing, capacity, tuck-ins, new geographies, systems). Those become the drumbeat.

➡ **Lender reporting.** If there's leverage, you'll have covenants and recurring bank packages. Accuracy and timeliness matter.

➡ **Audit and controls.** Many first-time sellers adopt auditor relationships, quarterly closes, and stronger internal controls. It's an upgrade, not a punishment—but it *is* an adjustment.

Treat this as infrastructure for scale. This will feel unnatural for a while—you'll adjust, just give it time.

New Roles, New Relationships

If you sold into an existing platform and now report to a platform CEO, you'll be building a new peer relationship. If you *are* the platform CEO, you'll be building a relationship with the board. Either way, the work is similar:

- Clarify decision rights early (what's yours vs. what's reserved for the board or others).
- Align on the VCP and the handful of metrics that define progress.
- Keep a steady "no surprises" rule—bad news early, with a plan.

Remember: you know the business best. Lead with that confidence and pair it with a tighter, more transparent operating rhythm.

Expect (Some) Turnover—and Manage It Well

Even in great cultures, some people won't want to make the shift from founder-led to investor-backed. Others aren't wired for the new pace or the added reporting. That's normal. Handle it cleanly and kindly:

- Identify the talent you need to keep and engage them meaningfully in the VCP.
- Where capability gaps exist, upgrade quickly and thoughtfully.
- Help good people who aren't a fit make graceful exits.

The goal isn't zero turnover; it's *healthy* turnover that strengthens the team for the next chapter.

Put a Support System in Place before You Need It

You don't white-knuckle your way through a transition like this. Build an ecosystem that covers the technical work of a deal and the human work of change.

Start with the core professional bench: a seasoned attorney to manage terms and protect you; a tax professional and financial advisor to map liquidity, diversification, and cash flow, and an estate planner to align the windfall with your family goals.

Then shore up the personal side. Talk early and honestly with your spouse or partner, your adult children (when appropriate), and any co-owners. Use your coach if you have one.. If you don't, find peer groups. CEO forums like Vistage, YPO/EO, Tiger 21, or your industry roundtable can be invaluable. Community won't make the decisions for you, but it will provide you support so that you can make thoughtful decisions.

Pre-Close Alignment for Post-Close Speed

Everything that creates value happens *after* the transaction. That's precisely why alignment must happen *before* it. If you're staying, insist on clarity around:

- The first 100-day plan and who owns what.
- The 12-month plan and resourcing (people, systems, capital).
- The three-to-five-year arc and the few levers that drive the return.
- Board cadence, reporting, and how decisions get made.
- Where the sponsor helps (and where they stay out of the way).

Do this work early and you'll compress the transition, steady the team, and step into the next chapter at a run rather than a wobble.

The First 100 Days: Stabilize, Communicate, Fortify

Day 1 to Day 100 is a tightening arc: close the books on the deal, close ranks with the team, and close gaps in controls. Think of it as three overlapping tracks:

- **Stabilize operations.** Confirm payroll, vendor payments, banking authorities, licenses, insurance, data security, and IT access. No surprises.

- **Communicate with intent.** Employees first, then customers, then partners. What's changing, what isn't, and why the future is bigger than the past.

- **Install the new cadence.** Weekly sponsor touchpoints, monthly KPI reviews, a clean Q1 close, and a written 12-month plan that rolls up to the five-year arc.

You can draft most of this before close. The more you front-load, the faster you move through the post-deal "hangover" and back into building mode.

Five Years, One Year at a time, One Quarter at a time

Typical hold periods run ~five years. That's the marathon. But you'll live it as a string of races: annual plans broken into quarterly priorities with owners, budgets, and dates. If the goal is a 3–5x cash-on-cash outcome, translate that into the few levers that actually move the needle for *your* business (pricing, mix, utilization, route density, same-store growth, add-on M&A, etc.). Write it down. Resource it. Report against it.

The Bottom Line

If you remember nothing else from this chapter, remember this: the emotional dip is normal; community reduces the amplitude; preparation shortens the duration. Put the right professionals around you, bring your family into the conversation early, and design your first 90 days post-close with as much intention as you designed the deal itself.

The Right Tool for the Right Job

By Ken Grider, Senior Managing Director, Raymond James

Private equity is a tool. Use it when the job calls for it. The job it's best at is unlocking growth you can see but aren't reaching on your own, like acquisitions you haven't pursued, capital your bank won't extend, a salesforce you haven't built, or new products and geographies you haven't entered.

I like to start thinking of how to use the tool with a simple exercise: *What's the true potential of this business if resources and energy weren't the constraint?* If you had the capital, the M&A muscle, the recruiting engine— what could this be? No one knows the answer better than you. Put it on paper.

Now you've got three doors.

Door One: Do nothing. You know there's headroom, but you leave it on the shelf.

Door Two: Articulate the headroom and sell. You're not the one to run the plan—and that's fine. But get credit for its value. Package the growth clearly so a strategic or a PE buyer can underwrite it. You'll monetize today and let someone else do the heavy lifting.

Door Three: Partner and go get it. Find a yin to your yang. You did the hard part—starting and proving the business. Bring in a partner that's great at the list you just wrote: stacking add-ons, raising outside capital, professionalizing the org, pushing into new markets and offerings. Negotiate the deal you want—minority or majority—and define your *highest and best use.* Maybe you protect culture, evaluate acquisitions, and help translate the vision while they handle the admin and scale mechanics. Make the last few years with your company fun again—and bigger.

That's when private equity shines.

Engineering a Great Outcome

Talk to real experts and get real advice. You'll find a lot of the early guidance from bankers and attorneys is effectively pro bono: they'll listen, ask sharp questions, and sketch a roadmap to earn the right to be your partner. Use that. But set a standard: in your very first meeting, you should learn something concrete about your industry, your path, and your specific hurdles. If someone plans to "learn the space" by using your company as a classroom, that's the wrong partner.

An ounce of planning here is worth a pound of cure. Assemble the functional working group early and make sure each seat knows what problem it owns. Bankers put the company in front of the right investors and choreograph the process. Lawyers make sure what's on paper matches what's been promised. Accountants keep everyone financially honest and realistic. Wealth advisors solve for *you*—the human who is about to move from one primary asset (your business) to a different life altogether.

And remember what actually makes a deal work. It isn't the deck, the model, or the glossy credentials. The rubber meets the road when the seller looks across the table and *believes*. Believes in the culture fit and the people. Believes the references. Believes that with this partner in, the probability of hitting the plan is higher than without them.

If you're rolling equity and staying in the seat for a run, that belief matters even more. The bankers c an slate the p ieces and t he numbers can sing, but the decision point is simple: *With this partner, do I see more potential and a better outcome—for me, my team, and the company—than I do alone?* If the answer is yes and you'll sleep better at night *having done the deal* than not, that's your green light.

Don't overlook the personal side. For most owners, the business is the income engine and the comfort blanket. A good transaction should de-risk your life: reduce or remove personal guarantees, move money outside the business, and replace that operating income with a more stable personal financial plan. The goal isn't just liquidity; it's confidence—feeling more secure post-transaction than you did when every payday depended on tomorrow's work orders.

Put those two pieces together and you've engineered a great outcome:

➡ **On the business side:** a partner who can unlock growth you wouldn't reach on your own—and a role that keeps you focused on your highest and best use.

➡ **On the personal side:** a plan that trades concentration risk for durable stability.

That's good finance and good stewardship.

One last reality check. If you make the growth list and you *can* execute it yourself—raise the capital, hire the leadership, integrate acquisitions, push into new markets—there may be *more* in it for you by going solo. But many owners prefer to wade in with a partner who brings the expertise and the conviction they don't yet have—and to take a few chips off the table along the way. There's no shame in that. It's smart.

Private equity is a tool. If the job is unlocking the growth you've mapped but haven't captured, it might be exactly the right one. If not, keep it handy in the tool belt and keep building.

Stop Mistaking Noise for a Market

By Michael Schodrof, Vice President, Raymond James

I see it all the time: business owners get comfortable because the phone won't stop ringing. Buy-side searchers. Junior associates "calling on behalf of" a fund. Folks working their own angle. The inbox fills up, and it starts to feel like, "I can hit a bid any time." That false confidence is the first mistake. Selling a company is not easy; it's a process—your process—and it takes real preparation.

Where I come in is before you answer those emails. Most owners need front-end planning and the right partners at the table. There are people who can help quantify two valuations: (1) what your company would be worth if it were buttoned-up and "perfect," and (2) what it's worth today. Their job is to help you close that gap. If you engage private equity before doing that work, you're negotiating from their starting point—a lower valuation that's easy to walk back. Get your house in order first, then go to market.

Build the Bench Before You Engage

Owners are often surprised by how many "boxes" exist in a serious sale process—and how unfamiliar those boxes are. The list isn't one-size-fits-all, but these roles come up again and again:

➡ **Tax**: a tax attorney or tax specialist (distinct from your auditor/CPA).

➡ **M&A Counsel**: a lawyer who lives in transaction documents, not general contracts.

➡ **Value Growth Accelerator**: the team that identifies the perfect vs. current valuation and helps close that gap.

➡ **General Counsel**: sometimes helpful to coordinate internal/legal readiness.

➡ **Wealth Advisor / Wealth Strategist**: to model outcomes and personal cash-flow.

➡ **Trust & Estate Attorney**: to align the transaction with your long-term plan.

Two Important Points About This Staging:

1. **Sequence matters.** Do the value-building work before you invite buyers in. You want the story and the numbers to match—your story, not theirs.

2. **Fit matters.** Some roles overlap. The goal isn't to build the biggest team; it's to assemble the right one for *your* process.

After the Wire: Don't Invest It All on Day One

Let's talk about what happens when the deal closes and the funds hit your account. Many owners are stepping into a pool of liquidity they've never seen before. It's normal for that to feel surreal. You don't have to deploy the capital immediately.

Three Practical Takeaways:

➡ **Plan early.** A couple of years out, we're already running the wealth plan, aligning trust and estate structures, and mapping post-close cash-flow.

➡ **Separate the business sale from the investment plan.** One is a transaction; the other is a long-term strategy. Don't let the urgency of the first rush the second.

➡ **Measure twice, cut once.** The right portfolio is built to your goals, not to a calendar.

The Through-Line

If you take nothing else from me, take this: the process is different for everybody. There is no universal checklist that, if you tick every box, guarantees the best outcome. But there *is* a universal mistake—confusing inbound noise with readiness. Your edge comes from preparation, sequencing, and surrounding yourself with pros who close the valuation gap *before* you invite bidders in.

Do that, and you'll walk into the room on your terms—clear on your numbers, clear on your team, and clear on how the proceeds will support the next chapter of your life.

EPILOGUE

By Jordan McMillian, Partner, Samson Partners Group

If you've learned one thing from this book, I hope it's this: Selling your business is one of the hardest decisions you will ever make, because it's not just about the money. It is personal. It is emotional. It is the moment when years of risk, sacrifice, and sweat are put under a microscope by strangers who think they know what it is worth. That is why so many owners, after the process is over, say the same thing: *"I wish I had been better prepared."*

Over the years, I've watched too many founders go into a sale with nothing more than good intentions and misplaced confidence. They thought timing would do the work. They thought the numbers would speak for themselves. They thought their legacy was obvious. But buyers saw risks they never addressed. Those founders walked away with regret—frustrated by the process, tied up in earnouts, or shortchanged on the price.

And yet I've also seen the other side. Founders who put in the work ahead of time. Who built the right systems. Who invited in the right counsel. Who humbled themselves enough to see their blind spots and fix them. Those founders closed on stronger terms, protected the people around them, and left with their legacy intact. They didn't just sell a business. They sold on their terms.

Why Samson Exists

That is the heart of why Samson was created. There are plenty of consultants who will sell you a framework and bill their hours. That is not what founders deserve. Samson was built to fight for the value you've created and to ensure the outcome reflects the years of sacrifice behind it.

We believe small and mid-sized businesses are the backbone of this country. When they thrive, communities thrive. When they grow, families prosper. And when they transition successfully, everyone benefits. Our measure of success is simple: did the founder walk away with pride and peace of mind?

What Makes Us Different

When Samson comes in, we don't start with slogans and spreadsheets. We start by getting inside the business. Sometimes that means stepping into the COO or CFO chair until the right hire is made. Sometimes it means building budgets and pipelines from scratch. Sometimes it means doing the small, unglamorous work no one else is willing to do.

And along the way, we tell the truth. Buyers will see risk where you don't. We'll point it out early and help you address it. That honesty can be uncomfortable. But it's also what strengthens the business and lifts valuation.

I'll never forget an owner who asked me to join full-time, sixty hours a week. Most advisors would have signed the contract and cashed the checks. I told him no. He didn't need me that much. What he needed was structure, discipline, and a handful of key processes. That honesty saved him hundreds of thousands of dollars and positioned him for a better exit. That is what Samson does: put the founder's outcome ahead of our own.

The Human Side

Numbers and processes matter, but trust matters more. Selling is not just technical. It is human. Letting outsiders into your business can feel threatening. We know that. That's why Samson invests in real relationships.

If you've spent time with Seth and our team at Sampson, you know what I mean. We are constantly connecting people. Always helping. Always coaching. A text from us might introduce you to someone you didn't know you needed. That generosity isn't strategy—it's who we are. And it's why founders who work with us don't just get an advisor. They get a partner who will stand with them through the most stressful transition of their careers.

Why This Book Matters

This book has not tried to make selling sound easy. It has tried to make it clear. It has shown you what buyers look for, where sellers stumble, and what separates a strong exit from a painful one.

If there is one thread running through every page, it is this: **preparation is everything.** Deals that appear effortless are the product of years of groundwork. The best outcomes go to founders who start early, face the hard truths, and shape their exit long before they meet a buyer.

A Final Word

You have heard the stories, seen the patterns, and been warned of the traps. The decision is now yours.

If you are serious about selling in the next three to five years—or even if you just want to know your true value—start now. Have the hard conversations. Put the right systems in place. Build your team. Seek wise counsel.

The journey will still be demanding. But it doesn't have to end with regret. Done right, it can end with pride, with peace, and with the satisfaction of knowing that the legacy you built will carry forward.

That is the future worth working for.

HIGHLIGHTS FROM THE EXIT VALUE REALIZATION SYSTEM™

Throughout this book, you've heard from founders, investors, and advisors who have lived through the private equity process. Beneath every story, there's a consistent pattern: value creation is not random. It follows structure.

The Exit Value Realization System (EVRS)™ was designed to help owners translate the lessons in these pages into a clear, repeatable framework for preparing, improving, and ultimately realizing the full value of their business.

Included here are EVRS™ highlights, distilling the core metrics, valuation drivers, and risk factors that private equity buyers use to evaluate companies. It's not theory; it's the scorecard investors apply every day. Use these to see your business through the investor's lens, identify your strongest foundations, and close the gaps that hold you back. Whether you're planning to sell in six months or six years, the goal is the same—to help you build a business that performs better now and commands the price it deserves when the time comes to sell.

FINANCIAL TRANSPARENCY

DESCRIPTION

- Refers to the clarity and openness of financial records and practices, including financial statements, accounting policies, and tax filings.

- Strong transparency means clear, accurate reporting, and easy access to the data used to create financial statements.

- Weak transparency can result in hidden risks, mismanagement, or misunderstandings that can hurt valuation.

WHY PRIVATE EQUITY CARES

- PE firms prefer businesses with strong financial transparency because it reduces risk during due diligence and post-acquisition.

- Transparency increases buyer confidence and ensures that all stakeholders have a clear understanding of the company's financial situation.

IMPACTS ON SELLER

- **High Transparency:** Higher valuation, as buyers feel confident that they have an accurate picture of the company's financial status.

- **Low Transparency:** Discounted valuation due to concerns over hidden financial risks, unclear reporting, or inconsistencies in financial practices.

- **Transparency Improvements:** Buyers may adjust the initial valuation if transparency improves but may still expect discounts until full clarity is established.

EXAMPLE

Factors	Weak	Medium	Strong
Financial Records	Poor or inconsistent historical data	Not fully standardized or updated	Clear, well-organized, and consistent
Valuation Impact	-15-30% discount	-10-15% discount	+0-10% premium
Buyer's Risk Perception	High	Moderate	Low

☸ CASH FLOW MANAGEMENT

DESCRIPTION

- Refers to the company's ability to effectively manage cash inflows and outflows to ensure it can meet its financial obligations.

- Strong cash flow management ensures the company has sufficient liquidity to cover operational costs, investments, and debt.

- Weak cash flow management can lead to financial strain, missed growth opportunities, or insolvency.

WHY PRIVATE EQUITY CARES

- PE firms look for businesses with strong cash flow management as it reduces financial risk and ensures the business can fund its operations and growth.

- Effective cash flow management makes it easier for a buyer to forecast future performance and supports post-acquisition investment plans.

IMPACTS ON SELLER

- **Strong Cash Flow Management:** Higher valuation due to predictable cash flow and financial stability.

- **Weak Cash Flow Management:** Lower valuation due to risks associated with liquidity issues, high debt levels, or inconsistent cash flow.

- **Cash Flow Improvements:** Buyers may offer a lower purchase price if cash flow is weak, but could be open to investing in improving liquidity post-sale.

EXAMPLE

Factors	Weak	Medium	Strong
Cash Flow Predictability	Erratic, difficult meetin obligations	Occasional liquidity issues	Stable & predictable
Valuation Impact	-15-30% discount	-10-15% discount	+0-10% premium
Buyer's Risk Perception	High	Moderate	Low

☸ Samson Partners Group

✗ BUDGETING & FORECASTING

DESCRIPTION

- Refers to the company's internal processes for managing and overseeing its financial operations, including budgeting, forecasting, and reporting.

- Strong financial controls ensure accuracy, regulatory compliance, and timely decision-making.

- Weak financial controls lead to errors, inefficiencies, and higher risks of fraud or non-compliance.

WHY PRIVATE EQUITY CARES

- PE firms prioritize strong financial controls to mitigate the risk of financial mismanagement and ensure the business is run efficiently.

- Reliable financial controls improve transparency and help the company maintain stable operations, reducing post-acquisition risks.

IMPACTS ON SELLER

- **Strong Financial Controls:** Higher valuation due to greater operational efficiency and reduced risk of errors or fraud.

- **Weak Financial Controls:** Discounted valuation due to the increased risk of inaccuracies, mismanagement, or compliance issues.

- **Control Improvements:** Buyers may initially offer a lower valuation, with the expectation that controls will be improved after acquisition.

EXAMPLE

Factors	Weak	Medium	Strong
Controls & Processes	Limited budgeting & no internal audits	Some budgeting & audits	Well-established & internal audits
Valuation Impact	-15-30% discount	-10-15% discount	+0-10% premium
Buyer's Risk Perception	High	Moderate	Low

QUALITY OF EARNINGS

DESCRIPTION

- Quality of earnings (QoE) refers to how accurately a company's reported earnings reflect its true financial health & sustainability.

- It's not just about revenue—earnings quality is influenced by cost structure, pricing power, customer retention, accounting practices, and operational efficiency.

- High-quality earnings come from core, repeatable operations, while low-quality earnings rely on one-time events or hidden risks.

WHY PRIVATE EQUITY CARES

- PE firms want to understand a business's true profitability, not just its top-line revenue.

- Poor-quality earnings can mask operational inefficiencies, unsustainable cost structures, or underinvestment.

- A business with high-quality earnings has stable margins, predictable cash flows, and resilience to economic shifts. This also gives lenders and investors more confidence in the PE firm and the deal.

IMPACTS ON SELLER

- **Higher Valuation:** Businesses with clean, reliable, and recurring earnings command higher EBITDA multiples.

- **Cost & Margin Analysis:** Buyers will assess pricing strategies, supplier relationships, and cost controls to ensure earnings are sustainable.

- **Adjustment to Price:** If earnings include temporary cost cuts, deferred expenses, or non-operating gains, buyers will adjust earnings downward, lowering valuation.

EXAMPLE

Factors	Low	Medium	High
Quality of Earnings	<50% of from core operations	50-80% from core operations	80%+ from core operations
Valuation Impact	-20-40% discount to EV	-5-15% discount to EV	+0-10% premium to EV
Buyer's Risk Perception	Low	Moderate	High

CUSTOMER CONCENTRATION

DESCRIPTION

- Customer concentration refers to the percentage of total revenue generated by a small number of customers.

- A business is considered concentrated if a single customer accounts for more than 15-20% of revenue or if the top ten customers account for more than 50%.

WHY PRIVATE EQUITY CARES

- High customer concentration increases risk—losing a key customer can significantly impact revenue and profitability.

- It affects cash flow predictability, making it harder to forecast future earnings and service debt obligations.

- Can signal a lack of diversification or customer dependency, reducing overall business resilience.

IMPACTS ON SELLER

- **Discounted Valuation:** A high-risk business with concentrated revenue often trades at lower EBITDA multiples.

- **Deal Structuring Issues:** PE firms may push for earnouts or seller financing to mitigate risk.

- **Post-Close Requirements:** PE firms may require seller involvement post-sale to maintain relationships.

EXAMPLE

Factors	Low	Medium	High
Customer Concentration	<20% Top 10 customers	20-50% Top 10 Customers	>50% Top 10 Customers
Valuation Impact	+0-10% of EV	-10-20% discount to EV	-20-40% discount to EV
Buyer's Risk Perception	Low	Moderate	High

CUSTOMER ATTRITION

DESCRIPTION

- Measures the rate at which customers leave or stop buying.

- High attrition or turnover means customers are less loyal, potentially indicating issues with service or value.

- Low turnover reflects customer satisfaction and a stable base.

WHY PRIVATE EQUITY CARES

- High turnover signals potential instability in revenue and profit streams.

- PE firms prefer businesses with high customer retention, as it indicates long-term sustainability and lower risk.

- High turnover increases customer acquisition costs and reduces profitability.

IMPACTS ON SELLER

- **Low Turnover:** Sellers may be able to command higher multiples and a smoother transaction process.

- **Medium Turnover:** Sellers might face moderate adjustments in valuation or earnouts depending on retention improvements.

- **High Turnover:** Sellers will likely see a significant discount in valuation, and buyers will require a higher degree of risk mitigation (such as price adjustments or contingency terms).

EXAMPLE

Factors	Low	Medium	High
Annual Retention	<60% retained	60-80% retained	+80% retained
Valuation Impact	20-40% discount to EV	-10-20% discount to EV	+0-10% of EV
Buyer's Risk Perception	High	Moderate	Low

REVENUE MIX, BACKLOG, & SUSTAINABILITY

DESCRIPTION

- **Revenue Mix:** The diversity of revenue sources. A balanced mix reduces risk and increases stability.

- **Backlog:** The total value of unfulfilled orders, showing future revenue potential.

- **Sustainability:** The long-term viability of revenue streams and market position. Sustainable businesses adapt to market changes and maintain stable cash flow.

WHY PRIVATE EQUITY CARES

- **Revenue Mix:** PE values diversified revenue for stability and growth. Heavy reliance on one product/customer adds risk.

- **Backlog:** A strong backlog indicates future revenue, reducing uncertainty and improving forecasting.

- **Sustainability:** PE prefers businesses that can weather market shifts and sustain long-term growth, as they offer predictable returns.

IMPACTS ON SELLER

- **High Stability:** Higher valuation, attractive to buyers with less perceived risk.

- **Moderate Stability:** Moderate discount, potential for adjustments based on future growth or operational risks.

- **Low Stability:** Significant discount due to future uncertainty and buyer concerns over risk.

EXAMPLE

Factors	Low	Medium	High
Revenue Stability	<10% fluctuatio	10-25% fluctuatio	>25% fluctuatio
Valuation Impact	+0-10% of EV	-10-20% discount to EV	-20-40% discount to EV
Buyer's Risk Perception	Low	Moderate	High

✦ ORGANIC GROWTH

DESCRIPTION

- Organic growth refers to the expansion of a business through its existing operations, such as increasing sales, expanding product offerings, or gaining market share.

- Key indicators of organic growth include revenue growth, customer retention, improved operational efficiency, and the ability to scale without relying on acquisitions or external factors.

WHY PRIVATE EQUITY CARES

- PE firms value organic growth because it demonstrates sustainable, long-term business health.

- It shows that the company can generate consistent revenue without the complexities or risks of acquisitions.

- Strong organic growth indicates that the company has a solid foundation, with efficient processes and loyal customers.

IMPACTS ON SELLER

- **High Organic Growth:** Higher valuation due to consistent and predictable growth.

- **Low Organic Growth:** Discounted valuation due to concerns about stagnation or over-reliance on external growth factors.

- **Improved Organic Growth:** Buyers may raise the valuation upward if recent growth shows a positive trend, especially with stronger sales or improved customer retention.

EXAMPLE

Factors	Weak	Medium	Strong
Growth Potential	Limited, struggling to expand	Moderate growth	High growth innovation & market share
Valuation Impact	-15-30% discount	-10-15% discount	+0-10% premium
Buyer's Risk Perception	High	Moderate	Low

MANAGEMENT EXPERIENCE & STRENGTH

DESCRIPTION

- Refers to the leadership team's expertise, depth, track record, and ability to drive the company's strategy and operations.

- Strong management ensures growth and operational efficiency, while weak or inexperienced leadership increases risk and potential instability.

- Leadership residing solely with the owner also increases the business's risk profile.

WHY PRIVATE EQUITY CARES

- PE firms prioritize capable leadership to manage growth, mitigate risks, and ensure long-term success.

- Experienced management teams reduce perceived risk, increasing buyer confidence.

IMPACTS ON SELLER

- **Strong Leadership:** Higher valuation due to confidence in execution.

- **Weak Leadership:** Lower valuation due to concerns over future performance and management instability.

- **Leadership Gaps:** Possible discount due to perceived risks of leadership transition.

EXAMPLE

Factors	Weak	Medium	Strong
Experience	<5 years average tenure	5-10 years average tenure	10+ years average tenure
Valuation Impact	-20-40% discount to EV	-10-20% discount to EV	+0-10% of EV
Buyer's Risk Perception	High	Moderate	Low

Samson
Partners Group

⊗ COMPANY CULTURE

DESCRIPTION

- Refers to the shared values, beliefs, and behaviors that shape how employees interact and work together.

- A strong culture promotes collaboration, high performance, and employee retention, while a weak culture can lead to inefficiencies, high turnover, and low employee satisfaction.

- It can be measured using employee retention rate.

WHY PRIVATE EQUITY CARES

- PE firms prioritize company culture because a strong, positive culture contributes to employee satisfaction, performance, and retention, all of which affect the company's value and future growth.

- A positive culture reduces operational risks and helps the company adapt to changes and challenges more effectively.

IMPACTS ON SELLER

- **Strong Culture:** Higher valuation due to the business's ability to retain talent and execute efficiently.

- **Weak Culture:** Lower valuation due to concerns over high turnover, low morale, and inefficiency.

- **Cultural Misalignment:** Potential discount if the company's culture is misaligned with potential buyers' values or expectations.

EXAMPLE

Factors	Weak	Medium	Strong
Employee Retention Rate	<60% annually	60-80% annually	80%+ annually
Valuation Impact	-20-40% discount to EV	-10-20% discount to EV	+0-10% of EV
Buyer's Risk Perception	High	Moderate	Low

SUCCESSION PLANNING

DESCRIPTION

- Succession planning refers to the strategies and processes a company has in place to identify and develop future leaders, ensuring a smooth transition when key personnel leave.

- A solid succession plan ensures business continuity, reducing disruption from leadership changes, and protecting the company's value post-acquisition.

WHY PRIVATE EQUITY CARES

- PE firms look for businesses that have a clear succession plan to avoid leadership gaps, which can disrupt operations and decrease the company's value.

- A well-prepared succession plan indicates stability and reduces the perceived risk of leadership transition after the acquisition.

IMPACTS ON SELLER

- **Well-Defined Succession Plan:** Higher valuation due to buyer confidence in leadership stability and continuity.

- **Lack of Succession Plan:** Potential discount due to perceived risks of leadership disruption and the need for an immediate leadership transition.

- **Uncertain Leadership Transition:** Possible delay in the sale or discount if a suitable leadership transition plan is not in place or is unclear.

EXAMPLE

Factors	Weak	Medium	Strong
Leadership Transition	No plan or clear successor	A plan in place but some gaps	Clear plan in place
Valuation Impact	-20-40% discount to EV	-10-20% discount to EV	+0-10% of EV
Buyer's Risk Perception	High	Moderate	Low

Samson Partners Group

OPERATIONS

DESCRIPTION

- Refers to the efficiency, scalability, and consistency of a company's day-to-day operations.

- Strong operational quality is demonstrated by streamlined processes, cost control, and the ability to scale without compromising quality.

- Weak operations lead to inefficiencies, poor customer satisfaction, and increased costs.

WHY PRIVATE EQUITY CARES

- PE firms value businesses with high operational efficiency because it drives profitability, scalability, and the ability to manage growth.

- Well-run operations reduce risk, making the business more attractive to potential buyers.

IMPACTS ON SELLER

- **Strong Operations:** Higher valuation due to scalability, efficiency, and lower risk.

- **Weak Operations:** Lower valuation due to perceived inefficiencies, higher risk, and increased cost structure.

- **Operational Improvements:** Potential for a buyer to invest in operational improvements post-acquisition, but the company may be valued lower due to current inefficiencies.

EXAMPLE

Factors	Weak	Medium	Strong
EBITDA Margin Stability	<10% EBITDA Margin	10-15% EBITDA Margin	+15% EBITDA Margin
Valuation Impact	-20-40% discount to EV	-10-20% discount to EV	+10-30% of EV
Buyer's Risk Perception	Low	Moderate	High

Samson
Partners Group

REPORTING

DESCRIPTION

- Refers to the accuracy, consistency, and timeliness of a company's financial and operational reporting.

- Strong reporting systems provide reliable, actionable insights that help drive decision-making and enable quick identification of issues.

- Weak reporting leads to poor decision-making, missed opportunities, and a lack of transparency, which can raise concerns during due diligence.

WHY PRIVATE EQUITY CARES

- PE firms value businesses with robust reporting systems because they provide clarity and transparency into financial performance, operations, and key business metrics.

- High-quality reporting reduces operational risk, improves forecasting, and instills buyer confidence.

IMPACTS ON SELLER

- **Strong Reporting:** Higher valuation due to confidence in accurate data, effective decision-making, and transparent financials.

- **Weak Reporting:** Lower valuation due to the perceived risk from unreliable or inconsistent data, potential for hidden problems, and delays in addressing them.

- **Reporting Improvements:** A potential buyer may see opportunities for improving reporting, but a business with weak reporting will face initial valuation discounts.

EXAMPLE

Factors	Weak	Medium	Strong
Data Accuracy	Unreliable Data	Some delays & inconsistencies	Highly accurate data that drives decisions
Valuation Impact	-15-30% discount	-10-15% discount	+0-10% premium
Buyer's Risk Perception	High	Moderate	Low

TECH STACK

DESCRIPTION

- Refers to the technology and systems in place that support the business's operations, growth, and innovation.

- A strong tech stack includes modern, scalable technologies that enable automation, security, and data-driven decision-making.

- A weak tech stack relies on outdated systems, manual processes, and increases vulnerability to cybersecurity risks.

WHY PRIVATE EQUITY CARES

- PE firms prioritize a modern tech stack because it supports operational efficiency, scalability, and future growth.

- A strong tech infrastructure reduces the risk of costly system upgrades or cyberattacks post-acquisition and facilitates data-driven decision-making.

IMPACTS ON SELLER

- **Modern Tech Stack:** Higher valuation due to scalability, reduced risks, and data-driven operations.

- **Outdated Tech Stack:** Lower valuation due to perceived risks and potential costs for upgrades or security issues.

- **Tech Investment Needs:** Potential for a lower initial valuation, but the buyer sees an opportunity for tech improvements post-sale.

EXAMPLE

Factors	Weak	Medium	Strong
Cost to Upgrade	>$500k	$0-500k	$0 to negligible
Valuation Impact	Becomes working capital expenditure	Becomes working capital expenditure	No impacts to EV
Buyer's Risk Perception	High	Moderate	Low

Where Are You Today? Where Do You Want to Go? Take the EVRS™ Assessment

If you're ready to see where your company stands today, scan the QR code to take the **EVRS™ Assessment**. You'll receive a quick snapshot of your business through the same lens investors use, helping you understand your strengths, risks, and next steps toward achieving the sale you want.

We don't provide a formal valuation: there's simply too much nuance involved for that. Instead, this tool is designed to help you apply what you've learned in this book to gauge where you are today and identify the areas worth investing in before you consider a sale.

Assessments like this can be challenging, and they're never perfect. We recommend taking it yourself and sharing it with someone independent who understands your business and, ideally, has been through an exit of their own. If you get stuck on a question, skip it or reach out to us. You're not alone in this process.

The goal isn't to simply score your business, but to spark clarity. No tool can capture every nuance, and we don't want to overstep or oversimplify. We simply want to give you something practical that helps you put all the pieces together. Take the assessment, see where you stand, and begin shaping the path to the exit you want.

No matter what, **get help**. Talk to advisors, talk to peers, and lean on those who've been there before. We care deeply about founders, and our only goal is to help you build the future you deserve.

www.ingramcontent.com/pod-product-compliance
Lightning Source LLC
Chambersburg PA
CBHW071200210326
41597CB00016B/1616